The Rugby Leagu

GU00889819

Contents

Preface

The Rugby League Year 1990/91 covers the main stories and results from a great season of British Rugby League. The facts are presented in a week-by-week format, and you can see how some of the more intriguing episodes developed. We leave it to you, to decide who stuck to their words and who produced 'the goods' when they were needed.

A full list of results is given for each week; 'mw' denotes a mid-week game, and 'bh' denotes a Bank Holiday encounter. League tables are shown for the First Division and the top fourteen clubs in the Second Division to include the results of each week's games.

John Gallagher, who joined Leeds from Rugby Union at the start of the season, reviews his first year in the professional code and looks forward to the coming season. You can join him and form your own views with the help of the full 1991/92 fixture tables.

Full of interesting information, **The Rugby League Year 1990/91** will provide you with an enlightening and amusing read. As a source of information, it is an essential addition to the libraries of all those with an interest in the game, and will prove a useful reference tool for seasons to come.

The
Rugby League
Year
1990/1

The Rugby League Year 1990/91

First Published 1991 by R&B Publishing, PO Box 200, Harrogate HG2 9RB

ISBN   1-873668-00-7

Printed and bound in Great Britain by Unwin Brothers Woking

British Library Cataloguing-in-Publication Data:
A catalogue record for this book is available
from the British Library

John Gallagher Reviews His First Year

In 1990 John Gallagher signed to Leeds RLFC for a record fee. Previously John had been playing Rugby Union for the world famous New Zealand All Blacks whom he helped win the Inaugural World Cup. He finally with whom capped his long list of Union achievements by being voted International Player of the Year in 1990. Here John gives his opinions on his first season in the professional code and looks forward to the new season.

For me, the highlight of the season was undoubtedly the Test series against Australia, which provided some of the best publicity Rugby League has seen for many years. Not only did over 50,000 go to Wembley for the first match, but many thousands more were able to watch it live on BBC TV. A very strong Australian side were convincingly beaten and caused a real surprise for the form book. It was great to watch, with Ellery Hanley, Garry Schofield and of course Paul Eastwood playing blinders.

The second test showed that the visitors had lost any complacency which they may have had in the first, and Mal Meninga's injury time try kept the Ashes tournament alive. At Elland Road, the wet weather seemed to quell the atmosphere a bit and the game seemed a lot tighter than the first two. Great Britain did not play badly, but Australia just seemed to close everything down with tight defence work. Ellery seemed to have a least four or five players onto him every time he touched the ball. As a series, I thought it was brilliant and Rugby League, was made the main topic of conversation by sports watchers around the country.

The domestic season's form teams were always going to be Wigan and Widnes. The Charity Shield's move to Swansea seemed more of a Welsh homecoming than a Rugby match for Jonathan Davies, and he was able to give a triumphant display in his home country. Even though Wigan were not at full strength, people began to ask if their bubble had burst and if it was to be Widnes' season. Wigan's first league match was a draw with Sheffield Eagles and when they lost to Widnes in the Lancashire Cup it did not look good for the form side of last season. However, they came good in the end their Championship triumph stands up as a lesson to us all - never give up until the whistle goes. Ellery Hanley shone through as Wigan's outstanding player even though he was surrounded by a team of excellent players. He would also be my choice of player of the year.

Widnes, who had seemed so strong at the start hit a bad patch later on and were pipped at the post to the Championship. They probably deserved to win a trophy but were twice the runners-up in the Championship and in the First Division Premiership. Jonathan Davies had an exceptional season, and although he played a few positions centre seemed to be his best.

Hull had a great start, and this was shown by the fact that they had four players in the test squad. Speculation centred on whether the loss of Brian Smith would mean they would founder, but the depth of talent in their squad kept them going. New coach, Noel Cleal, must have been more than happy when Hull took the Premiership. A lot of their success appeared to be due to an excellent halfback pairing of Patrick Entat and Greg Mackie, backed up by Karl Harrison in the forwards.

Castleford won the Yorkshire cup and then seemed to have a slow start in the league. However, before anyone seemed to notice, they were confounding their critics by being top of the league and in contention for the title. As a team they have very solid forwards with Graham Steadman excelling.

Leeds' season was showing that the Aussies could be pushed, when we gave them a scare on a perfect day at Headingley. We went 10 points up, but in the end succumbed to some last minute action from the great Australian captain, Mal Meninga. In the League, we proved to be a real Jekyll and Hyde team. We suffered from a massive amount of pre-season hype, and public expectation was high, which unfortunately we did not live up to. The loss of three early games gave us an uphill task despite the sterling efforts of our best player, Garry Schofield.

St Helens had an inconspicuous season, but with a few highlights; like when they beat Widnes in the semi-final of the Challenge Cup. They looked to be falling apart in the actual final but recovered in the second half to give themselves credit in a game which Wigan always seemed to have under control. Their outstanding player for me was Jonathan Griffiths whilst George Mann also had a good season.

Bradford Northern showed everybody how to beat Wigan in the league with a tremendous 31-30 victory, but they failed to launch a serious bid on the title by inconsistent play. Most of their highlights came before Christmas when they beat Wigan again, this time in the Regal Trophy, and went on to reach the final. My choice of best player for them is the second rower John Hamer.

Featherstone did not stand out this season although they did have a good run of wins towards the end, managing to beat Bradford and take a place in the Premiership. Deryck Fox and Brendan Tuutu stood out as their best players.

Warrington at one stage in the season were playing top class rugby but seemed to sink lower and lower in the division. However they managed to surface again by winning the Regal Trophy and put in a good mid-season rally. Consistency was again a problem. Their ex-union half back Kevin Ellis was their best player.

Wakefield reached the final of the Yorkshire Cup and beat Wigan and Hull at home, but they were always on the verge of relegation. Their outstanding player was Adrian Shelford.

Hull KR had a good start to the season, always in the upper echelons of the league. After Christmas they seemed to find it hard to win any games and they did not manage to avoid relegation. Tony Sullivan gets my vote as their best player.

Sheffield Eagles must be one of the most unlucky teams. At both the start and end of season they were excellent but they let themselves down mid-season. They had a memorable win against Wigan, but this all goes to show how tough things are in the first division when you can beat the best but still go down. For me, Sam Panapa stood out as their outstanding player.

Oldham were a very hard team to beat and didn't deserve relegation after reaching the semi finals of the Challenge Cup. Charlie McAllister was their best player. Rochdale were on the receiving end of a lot of hidings. Their one win, against Bradford, proved to be a flash in the pan. Their fullback, Colin Whitfield appeared to have a good season.

Looking ahead to the 1991/92 League season and the new three division system. In the first division all teams have got to raise their form to beat Wigan. Though, let's not forget that every team lost last year. Even the top teams could be, and were, beaten. Everybody has shown what they can do on the day, the secret lies in consistency. Every season looks like it's going to be tougher than the one before and this one is no exception. All players also have an additional target, being selected for the Great Britain side to tour Australia in the Summer of 1992. The next Ashes test in Australia will be a stormer, as British Rugby has improved so much the Aussies know that we are a force to be reckoned with.

Of the newly promoted teams, I only have experience of playing Halifax so it is hard to judge how they will all perform in the first division. Halifax's quarter-final appearance in the Challenge Cup bodes well and I hope they can keep at bay the financial problems which haunted them in 1990. Newly promoted teams can often upset the established teams early on, so no one will be taking fixtures against Salford and Swinton lightly.

The second division will be a tough place from now on. Any team promoted from there will be good opposition, and I think there will be a lot more interest in the second division than before. I am not sure how the third division will be viewed, I hope it does not get forgotten.

I am often asked if I think Rugby League suffers because only a few clubs seem to win the trophies and therefore appear to dominate the game. I think it is the opposite. The Great Britain side has much to thank clubs like Wigan and Widnes for. It is they who provide talented International players who can compete at the highest level, and allow the country to hold its head high. Other teams should aim for these high standards, rather than waiting for Wigan to lose players and come down to their level. There is no reason why excellence in one team should not force everyone up to that standard. That would be good for the game and spectators.

The new season will also provide many of the Welsh players a chance to don their country's shirt once again when they play the touring Papua New Guinea team. A lot of them have already played at full international level in Rugby Union. I am sure wearing the Welsh jersey again will give them a lot of pride. Hopefully it will show that Rugby League is not just a game played by Englishmen. Davies, Devereaux, Young, Griffiths, Ford and Cordle, would all be useful on any Great Britain side, and I would not like to bet on a result in an England v Wales match.

My Union days have shown me the importance of playing in and against different countries. Rugby League is still centred in the North of England and in Australia so there is lot of room for expansion. More schools need to play and more international tours need to be arranged to help this process along, like the recent visit to Russia. There still does not seem to be a lot of awareness of what is going on in Rugby League in the south of Britain, but I am sure when the Great Britain side return with the Ashes next summer this will really enhance the awareness process.

August 18th - August 24th

RESULTS

ROUNDUP

Union convert Jonathan Davies, returned to Wales and scored the first hat-trick of tries in his Rugby League career, as he helped *Widnes* defeat *Wigan* to win the Charity Shield for a record third time in succession. Swansea, the heart of Welsh Rugby Union had been chosen as the venue for the Charity Shield in an attempt to spread Rugby League in South Wales. The 11,178 that turned up at Vetch Field in miserable conditions saw Davies, who also scored two goals, pick up the man-of-the-match award.

Wigan took the lead after only five minutes when Frano Botica, the newly signed All Black stand-off, kicked an easy goal. Widnes didn't hit back until the 29th minute when Tony Myler capitalised on good work by John Devereux to put Davies over for his first try.

Just before half-time, it was again Myler who linked well with Andy Currier, this time to help Devereux score. Davies added the goal to give Widnes a 10-2 lead at the interval. Tongan forward Emosi Koloto made a brilliant break to set Martin Offiah off for one of his typical tries in the corner after only seven minutes of the second half. Five minutes later Davies ran on to a Shaun Edwards up-and-under and continued to sprint 80 yards for a spectacular try which he then goaled. Davies grabbed his third try after 61 minutes following a strong run by Alan Tait, before Frano Botica popped up again to score a consolation try for Wigan, and then went on to kick his second goal.

Sheffield's scrum-half Mark Aston dominated the scrums and a large part of the action when the two first division clubs *Bradford Northern* and the Eagles met in the Preliminary Round of the Yorkshire Cup.

However, it was Northern that came away with the honours thanks largely to a disallowed try. The Bradford team were already lined up under the posts after Mark Gameson had swept over from a neat diagonal run to claim a try. But, after consulting a linesman, the referee cancelled the try and sent off Sheffield's Sonny Nickle for elbowing Bradford's Tony Marchant.

Instead of being 2-14 down, Northern rushed to the other end for a penalty, to go in only 4-8 down at half time. In the second half their pack seemed much more interested and an outstanding performance by forward Karl Fairbank helped Northern's kicker David Cooper, the powerful Ian Wilkinson, and speed-man Gerald Cordle to score tries.

Salford showed their determination for the coming season with an easy win over the *Rochdale Hornets*. Adrian Hadley signalled the start of Salford's attack by running in a try in the first few minutes of the morning kick-off game. Rochdale were on the rack for most of the rest of the game and suffered from a total of seven tries, six goals and one drop goal.

Hull K.R. performed a demolition job on *Nottingham* in their preliminary round game. A thundering display by the Humbersiders produced 18 tries and 14 goals that were only answered by one converted try. The massacre emphasised the growing gulf between the first and the second divisions, and brought renewed calls for a three division system to be introduced.

Carlisle won the BNFL Cumbria cup for the first time in their history by beating *Workington*. The only drawback for a delighted Carlisle coach, Cameron Bell, was the dismissal of Kiwi centre Brad Hepi for landing a knock-out punch in an off-the-ball incident involving Workington's Paul Penrice.

Welsh National Team Revival

Following the success of the Charity Shield in Swansea, there was renewed talk of re-starting the Welsh National squad. This prompted the Rugby League to announce firm plans to relaunch the Welsh side after an eight season gap. One of their aims was for Wales to compete in the 1995 Centenary World Cup, even though it would rob Great Britain of some of its star players.

Fulham - Down Under

Fulham coach Ross Strudwick announced that he would like an all-Australian squad to face teams from the North. The revolutionary idea was announced as a plan to get more people through the turnstiles. Adding a 'novelty' value to each game would encourage visiting fans and attract the large number of Australians resident in the capital, to home matches.

Cogger Back in Oldham Fold

Oldham's Australian rebel, John Cogger, who had disappeared for four months, confirmed that his dispute with the club was over. He said he would be returning to complete his contract, and help Oldham now they had returned to the first division.

No Increase at Trafford

Trafford Borough were refused special permission by the League to increase their quota of overseas players above three. Despite being in a development area it was decided that Trafford were not divorced from the heartland of Rugby League like Fulham, Nottingham and Carlisle.

Russian Visit Delayed

The Rugby League's special promotional tour of the Soviet Union with Ryedale-York and Leigh was postponed for a year because of the success of Rugby League in the Soviet Union.
   The Soviet's said that they were expecting to have their own professional championship starting in the spring of 1991, and would prefer the tour at the end of May 1991 to boost the impact of the championship.

Halifax New Lease of Life

Financially troubled second division club Halifax were given a reprieve from liquidation when a new consortium made a better offer to the club's creditors. The decision ended a month of uncertainty for the players, but resulted in the sacking of Scott Rawlinson who refused to sign a new deal. The new board appointed ex-Bradford and Keighley centre, Peter Roe, as coach.

25th August - 31st August

RESULTS

YORKSHIRE CUP - 1st Round

Batley	17	Huddersfield	10
Dewsbury	26	Keighley	14
Doncaster	4	Halifax	40
Featherstone	36	Bramley	4
Hull	6	Castleford	10
Leeds	16	Bradford	24
Ryedale-York	0	Hull K.R.	10
Wakefield	28	Hunslet	18

LANCASHIRE CUP - 1st Round

Carlisle	38	Workington	18
Fulham	50	Runcorn	0
Leigh	26	Swinton	6
Salford	27	Oldham	24
St Helens	56	Trafford	24
Warrington	36	Chorley	8
Whitehaven	6	Widnes	70
Wigan	70	Barrow	8

ROUND-UP

In the Yorkshire Cup first round; John Gallagher's first class debut appeared to be going according to the script when *Leeds* took a 16-8 lead early in the second half of this clash, until a determined *Bradford Northern* side picked it up and tore it to shreds. The Leeds full-back and former All-Black who was signed in the close-season for a reported £350,000 described his first really competitive match as "Bloody Hard" and said he was glad to get it "out of the way" following the endless publicity since his signing. Bradford's loose-forward Paul Medley and scrum-half Mark Wilson, both ex-Leeds players, were the main undoers of their old club. Wilson dominated the scrum-half dual with Harkin whilst Medley used his strength and speed to break apart the Leeds defence and managed to grab two tries for himself.

Castleford narrowly defeated *Hull* in a clash that never really lived up to expectations at the Boulevard. Hull appeared to be short of imagination but they made Castleford, who looked to be cruising to victory, endure a frantic last 15 minutes to hang on to victory.

Halifax, still celebrating their financial survival, had more to celebrate when Colin Atkinson landed a hat trick to help them beat *Doncaster*. *Featherstone* had an easy win against *Bramley* with a seven try blitz. *Hull KR* dominated the game but only managed to put 10 points past *Ryedale-York*.

Wakefield came back from a shock three point deficit at half-time to overturn *Hunslet*. Two young players, Dean Hall and Nathan Grahem helped *Dewsbury* to defeat *Keighley* and newly appointed coach Barry Seabourne saw his *Huddersfield* side lose to a fighting display from *Batley*.

In the Lancashire Cup first round; Last years beaten finalists went out in the first round when second division *Salford* held off an *Oldham* revival to notch up a 27-24 victory at the Willows. Tony Barrow's newly promoted side were 20-8 behind at one stage only to fight their way back and to take the lead for the first time in the 63rd minute. However, despite having lost stand-off David Fell with concussion, Salford spurred themselves into action and clinched victory in controversial circumstances after 72 minutes. Loose-forward Andy Burgess swooped on a loose ball, for his second try of the match, when Salford substitute Frank Cassidy appeared to have knocked on and Oldham seemed to hesitate waiting for the decision.

Widnes and *Wigan* both ran up cricket scores of 70 points apiece to defeat *Whitehaven* and *Barrow* respectively. Jonathan Davies followed up his Charity Shield hat-trick with four tries and nine goals, whilst Wigan had 12 of their Cup winning team on display to slaughter their newly relegated visitors.

Leigh managed a late surge of three tries to spare their blushes after leading *Swinton* by only 10-6 nearing full-time. Cup holders *Warrington* were under-strength but still managed an easy win at *Chorley*. *Carlisle* beat *Workington* for the second time in two weeks after winning the Cumbria Cup the previous week. *St Helens* ran in 56 points against *Trafford* but still showed some defensive gaps to concede 24 points. Londoners *Fulham* had an easy win over struggling *Runcorn*.

Heavy Talk

The Australian Kangaroos followed the announcement of a £250,000 sponsorship deal with Castlemaine XXXX by claiming that they will bring over a squad with an average weight of 16 stones. They also claimed that they were going to repeat the clean sweeps that they made in 1982 and 1986.

On or Off?

Leigh Miners' player Alan Draper came on as substitute in their match against Saddleworth in the Opencast National League, then 15 seconds later, he was sent off for a dangerous tackle.

Covet Thy Neighbour

Martin Offiah was named as the man that most coaches would like in their team. First Division coaches were asked to pick their best team with the restriction that they couldn't pick any of their own players. Martin Offiah gained 10 votes from a possible 13, Alan Tait and Kevin Iro gained 9 and Kelvin Skerrett 8.

The top team would be: 1. Alan Tait, 2. Des Drummond, 3. Andy Currier, 4. Joe Lydon, 5. Martin Offiah, 6. Shaun Edwards, 7. Andy Gregory, 8. Kevin Ward, 9. Phil McKenzie, 10. Adrian Shelford, 11. Mike Gregory or Andy Platt, 12. Ron Gibbs, 13. Ellery Hanley.

Runcorn Further Troubles

Runcorn Highfield found themselves in new trouble, this time off the pitch, when they decided to leave their ground after their rent was doubled. St Helens Town soccer club was chosen as their new home, only to have an official complaint made against them by St Helens RLFC who thought that the move was not in the best interest of the game.

Wigan Favourites

Wigan were named as favourites to retain their First Division title at 5-4, with premiership holders Widnes at 11-4 and high spending Leeds at 3-1. Leigh were made 4-5 favourites to win the Second Division and bounce straight back up into the First Division, with Salford at 5-2 and Halifax 8-1.

Another Ban

Alan Rathbone, who was banned from the professional game after claiming that several Warrington players were on drugs, was banned from the Warrington Amateur League. The match that he was going to play in however, Crossfields versus Latchford Albion, was abandoned in the second half when Latchford had three players sent off.

1st September - 7th September

RESULTS

YORKSHIRE CUP - 2nd Round

Bradford 12	Castleford 42		
Dewsbury 18	Batley 8		
Featherstone 22	Hull KR 31		
Wakefield 26	Halifax 17		

LANCASHIRE CUP - 2nd Round

Carlisle 7	Warrington 28
Leigh 40	Fulham 8
Salford 21	St Helens 7
Widnes 24	Wigan 22

ROUNDUP

In the Lancashire Cup; Jonathan Davies again proved the king pin in *Widnes'* second win over *Wigan* before the championship games even got under way. With only four minutes to go to full time, Davies ran in a try to level the scores at 22-22. He then cooly took his pressure kick from the touchline to nudge Widnes into the lead and to bring his personal points total to 66 in just three games. Altogether the lead changed hands eight times in this thrilling match which contained everything from overhead passes to dropped interceptions. Tries from Offiah and Devereux proved enough with Davies' kicking for a 14-10 half-time lead over Wigan who had scored through Goodway and three Lydon penalties. After 48 minutes Platt sent Dean Bell in for a well deserved try and a Lydon kick put Wigan back into the lead. Davies then took two penalties when Shaun Edwards strayed offside and when Hampson was sin-binned with Tait after a clash of full-backs. Gregory and Davies' tries sealed the superbly balanced game.

Salford claimed a famous victory over *St Helens* to record a third first division scalp in their Lancashire Cup exploits. Although the game was delicately balanced early on, Salford gained the upper hand through sloppy play by Saints.

Ian Jeffrey and John Woods, the two *Leigh* centres, ensured a win over *Fulham* with five tries between them, three for Jeffrey and two for Woods. *Warrington* completed the semi-final line-up by beating *Carlisle*. The Cumbrian Cup holders had to play the second half without Clayton Friend who was making his return to the club and who was sent off five minutes before half-time.

In the Yorkshire Cup; *Hull Kingston Rovers* launched a terrific comeback for the Humbersiders to win their 'War of the Rovers' with *Featherstone*. Featherstone appeared to have the game all sewn up at half time when they went in with a 14-3 lead through tries from Casey, Banks and Manning plus a penalty from Deryck Fox. In the second half, however, the East Hull side staged a recovery. Greg Austin started the comeback when he re-gathered his own kick to score in the 50th minute. Prop Bryan Niebling then put Paul Speckman over and only two minutes later Anthony Sullivan scored from a 60 yard move to put Hull K.R. into the lead by a solitary point. Featherstone hit back with a try in the 72nd minute from Terry Manning when he took advantage of some very weak tackling to score his second try. Leading 22-19 Featherstone then seemed to relax a bit and the Humbersiders dominated the later part of the match. With only two minutes remaining, substitute Irvine took the ball from Speckman to score the winning try. Graeme Hallas scored his fifth goal to seal the game and a semi-final place for the Robins.

Holders *Bradford Northern* crashed out of the Cup in a re-located game at Bradford City's Valley Parade ground. *Castleford* threw the ball about at will, and took advantage of all Bradford's errors to have the match won by half-time.

Wakefield Trinity reached the semi-finals for the first time in seven years with a close win over *Halifax* who lacked any real aggression.

Dewsbury also reached the semi-finals with a sturdy display against their neighbours *Batley* in a game which had more than it's fair share of unforced errors.

Smith Returns to Australia

Hull's Australian Coach Brian Smith, announced he was going to resign in order to return to Australia and a coaching job at wealthy Sydney club St.George. He had been at Hull for two seasons and had taken them to the Premiership final 18 months previously.

Panthers Get Ready for Big Time

Gateshead Panthers were born with a five year plan to establish a professional team on Tyneside. Officials of the club, based at Gateshead Stadium, said that they hoped to break into the Second Division by 1995 and that they hoped to be entertaining the big crowds of the First Division within the decade.

Rombo Sidelined

Leeds' newly signed Kenyan winger Eddie Rombo was sidelined, and forced to miss some useful practice in Alliance games, because the paperwork for his work permit had not been sorted out properly.

Hornets Spending Spree

Rochdale Hornets continued their spending spree in an effort to stay in the first division with their signing of Australian forward David Gallagher. Hornets' total spending in the summer reached £250,000 with the deal.

Halifax Special Issue

Halifax announced that they wanted to raise more than £150,000 from their fans with the release of a special share issue. They wanted supporters to pledge £15 each, to help keep the club in business after their close call with The Receiver.

Runcorn OK

Runcorn Highfield's new headquarters at St Helens Town soccer ground were approved by 26 votes to 6 by the RL Council, despite disapproval from the RL Board and St Helens RLFC.

Ellery Best of 80's

Ellery Hanley collected the Rugby League 'Man-of-the-Decade' award. Lee Crooks collected the 'Most Memorable Goal' award for his goal that levelled the game and series against New Zealand at Elland Road in 1985. Garry Schofield got the 'Best Try' award and Joe Lydon the 'Best Drop Goal' award.

September 8th - September 14th

RESULTS

YORKSHIRE CUP - Semi-Final

Castleford 29	Hull KR 6 mw
Wakefield 25	Dewsbury 2 mw

LANCASHIRE CUP - Semi-Final

Salford 16	Leigh 7 mw
Widnes 20	Warrington 4 mw

DIVISION 1

Bradford 10	Widnes 14
Featherstone 14	Hull KR 14
Hull 20	St Helens 14
Oldham 32	Leeds 22
Wakefield 42	Rochdale 6
Warrington 30	Castleford 12
Wigan 18	Sheffield 18

DIVISION 2

Barrow 0	Salford 31
Batley 6	Leigh 22
Carlisle 50	Chorley 16
Doncaster 11	Hunslet 8
Halifax 38	Dewsbury 6
Huddersfield 26	Doncaster 24 mw
Keighley 26	Huddersfield 30
Ryedale-York 36	Nottingham 8
Swinton 40	Whitehaven 10
Trafford 20	Runcorn 12
Whitehaven 16	Halifax 8 mw
Workington 9	Fulham 4 mw

ROUNDUP

Captain of the Eagles, international Darral Powell, was the main driving and inspirational force behind a determined *Sheffield* side that earned a well deserved draw and produced the shock result of the opening day of the championship. Powell's performance overshadowed the long awaited return of Ellery Hanley for *Wigan*.

Leeds were looking to blow away the memories of their first round Yorkshire Cup exit to Bradford Northern with a strong performance against newly promoted *Oldham*. These hopes took a big blow when scrum-half Paul Harkin was dismissed for tripping after only 30 minutes by referee Robin Whitfield. Oldham took full advantage with scrum-half Mike Ford inspiring the Roughyeds to victory.

Featherstone and *Hull KR*, meeting for the second time already in the season played out a bad tempered draw at Post Office Road. Hull KR ended up with only 11 players on the pitch when skipper Bryan Niebling and full-back David Lightfoot got their marching orders.

Hull inflicted another defeat on a *St Helens* side that contained seven changes from the side that lost to Salford in the Lancashire Cup. Noel Cleal was playing for Hull only after a specialist told him that he could not cause any more damage to his already rebuilt wrist. Paul Eastwood scored three goals for Hull to take his scoring run to 24 successive games.

Wakefield Trinity zoomed to the top of the First Division by notching up 42 points in their victory over *Rochdale* at Bell-Vue. This victory was only achieved after Rochdale had claimed a six point lead in the first half hour.

Runcorn came close to recording their first victory in two seasons after leading *Trafford* by 12-6 at half time. However, they threw it away and Trafford kept up Runcorn's losing streak.

Coach Peter Roe locked the *Halifax* players in the changing rooms for a 20 minute talking to, after a display that he described as disgraceful when they lost to *Whitehaven*.

County Cup Semi-finals

Dewsbury went close to scoring a few times but they were shut out by Wakefield who strode through to the Yorkshire Cup Final in impressive style. Castleford claimed the other Final slot by almost completely outclassing Hull KR at home.

Widnes picked up a good win over the Lancashire Cup holders Warrington to become favourites for the final. Salford booked their place in the final, and celebrated the signing of a new sponsor, by adding the scalp of a useful Leigh side to their collection of First Division scalps in the cup.

Chicken Bone

Keighley's second-rower, David Nelson, was kept over in hospital in a very serious condition after choking on a chicken bone and losing a lot of blood. Two operations on his throat were not sufficient and a third was planned.

Wigan Injuries

Wigan said that they had no less than six first team injuries for their forthcoming game against Castleford on the coming week-end. The injury list included Kelvin Skerrett, the Bradford Northern prop, who signed to Wigan in the close season for a fee believed to be around £240,000 over three years. Skerrett had not completed a game, complaining of breathing difficulties.

Iro In Second Division

Former Wigan winger Tony Iro, 6ft and 16stone, joined Leigh on a short term contract from Australian club Manly. Iro had expressed a desire to learn the 'forwards game' and thought the British second division an ideal learning ground.

Kiss to Quit

Nicky Kiss, the former Wigan and Great Britain hooker, was forced to quit the game at the age of 30 on medical advice following a car crash. Kiss had hoped to make a comeback but tests had revealed spinal damage, and he was told that he risked permanent damage if he played again. Wigan had given Nicky a testimonial cheque for £30,000 as their longest serving player.

Discipline

David Lightfoot and Bryan Niebling, both of Hull K.R., were given four match suspensions for being sent off against Featherstone. Paul Harkin, however, was found 'not guilty' after the committee saw a video of him being dismissed for tripping against Oldham.

September 15th - September 21st

RESULTS

DIVISION 1			DIVISION 2	
Castleford 18	Wigan 38		Chorley 27	Hunslet 23
Hull KR 20	Warrington 14		Dewsbury 13	Carlisle 24
Leeds 22	Hull 24		Fulham 22	Barrow 8
Rochdale 20	Sheffield 24		Keighley 21	Batley 14
St Helens 24	Bradford 20		Leigh 6	Halifax 16
Wakefield 17	Oldham 12		Runcorn 10	Ryedale-York 22
Widnes 41	Featherstone 14		Salford 30	Workington 8
			Swinton 34	Bramley 19
			Trafford 52	Nottingham 4
			Whitehaven 11	Huddersfield 8

	P	Pts		P	Pts
Wakefield	2	4	Salford	2	4
Widnes	2	4	Trafford	2	4
Hull	2	4	Carlisle	2	4
Wigan	2	3	Swinton	2	4
Hull KR	2	3	Ryedale-York	2	4
Sheffield	2	3	Halifax	2	4
Warrington	2	2	Huddersfield	3	4
Oldham	2	2	Whitehaven	2	4
St Helens	2	2	Fulham	2	2
Featherstone	2	1	Leigh	2	2
Bradford	2	0	Keighley	2	2
Leeds	2	0	Doncaster	2	2
Castleford	2	0	Workington	2	2
Rochdale	2	0	Chorley	2	2

ROUNDUP

Wakefield staged a rally against *Oldham* to jump to the top of the first division. Despite losing their new signing Adrian Shelford, formerly of Wigan, with a leg injury after 10 minutes, Wakefield produced a rally on 50 minutes to score 12 points in a two minute blitz.

Inexplicable lapses of concentration near their own try line continued to be the main problem as *Leeds* tasted defeat for the third successive game, this time at home to *Hull*. On attack, however, they showed the potential that everybody is waiting to see unleashed.

Sheffield scored five tries to three in beating *Rochdale* and Mark Aston got two of them. *St Helens* defeated *Bradford Northern* in a match full of unforced errors at Knowsley Road, even though Bradford scored four tries to Saints' three.

A remarkable second half by *Widnes* saw off *Featherstone* who had led 6-3 at the break with two tries to Devereux and Eyres for Widnes. *Hull* produced a turn up for the books by beating *Warrington* in their evening game. *Wigan* eventually ran out easy winners over a poor *Castleford* defence.

Halifax had prop Brendan Hill to thank for punching through the gaping holes in the *Leigh* defence to score a win over the divisional favourites. *Dewsbury* gave away three tries through their own unforced errors to give *Carlisle* a victory.

In a bad tempered match at *Swinton*, two players were sent off and three were sin-binned as the home side defeated *Bramley*. *Huddersfield* lost their first game at *Whitehaven*. *Salford* were easy winners over *Workington* and *Trafford* overpowered *Nottingham* to go first and second in the division respectively.

Drummond Drama

Des Drummond of Warrington had a close scrape with death in the Wires' match with Hull KR. He swallowed his tongue which had become trapped behind his gumshield when he was elbowed on the neck. Luckily the Physios were quickly onto the pitch to save the writhing winger. Confused, Des tried to play on but he was brought off by the Wires' coach on the advice of the Hull KR doctor.

The King is Out

Australian skipper Wally Lewis was ruled out of the forthcoming tour through injury. Lewis led the Kangaroos in 20 games in Britain and France on their last tour four years previously.

Amateur Sponsorship

The Sports Council announced that they were to make a £640,000 grant available to support the British Amateur Rugby League Association's four year plan for development from 1990-94. BARLA chairman Alan Gibb said that it would provide a major boost in the build-up to the 1995 centenary year.

Broken Arm not Jaw

Warrington prop, Neil Harmon declared that he expected to be out of action for more than a month after breaking his arm in Warrington's defeat by Hull KR.

Meanwhile, Oldham's stand-off was given the all-clear after fears that he had broken his jaw in their match against Wakefield.

As Good as Goulding

Bobby Goulding received a severe reprimand, and was warned about his future conduct by the Rugby League's board of directors when he was found guilty of bringing the game into disrepute. He had been involved in a fight at an Auckland restaurant whilst on Great Britain's tour of NZ.

All ticket

Wigan became the first club to say that their match against the touring Australians was going to be an all-ticket game, with a 30,000 limit.

Cumbria

Alan Tait of Widnes and David Cairns of Barrow were the only two Great Britain players named in the Cumbrian squad to face the Australians at Workington on 12 October.

September 22nd - September 28th

RESULTS

YORKSHIRE CUP - Final

Castleford 11	Wakefield 8

DIVISION 1

Featherstone 24	Bradford 26
Hull 32	Widnes 6
Oldham 28	Castleford 22 mw
Sheffield 34	Wakefield 6 mw
St Helens 42	Hull KR 10
Warrington 10	Leeds 22
Wigan 24	Rochdale 2

DIVISION 2

Barrow 16	Leigh 32
Batley 10	Salford 21
Bramley 8	Halifax 56
Carlisle 44	Runcorn 13
Doncaster 38	Nottingham 14
Fulham 8	Whitehaven 30
Hunslet 17	Trafford 10 mw
Ryedale-York 42	Chorley 8
Swinton 22	Keighley 16
Workington 15	Dewsbury 9

	P	Pts
Hull	3	6
Wigan	3	5
Sheffield	3	5
Wakefield	3	4
St Helens	3	4
Widnes	3	4
Oldham	3	4
Hull KR	3	3
Leeds	3	2
Warrington	3	2
Bradford	3	2
Featherstone	3	1
Castleford	3	0
Rochdale	3	0

	P	Pts
Halifax	4	6
Carlisle	3	6
Ryedale-York	3	6
Salford	3	6
Swinton	3	6
Whitehaven	4	6
Trafford	3	4
Doncaster	3	4
Leigh	3	4
Huddersfield	3	4
Workington	3	4
Keighley	3	2
Fulham	3	2
Chorley	3	2

ROUNDUP

A disputed match-winning try by *Castleford's* David Plange took the Yorkshire Cup back to Castleford after a close and exciting match at Elland Road. Plange, making his first appearance for Castleford this season, also produced a try saving tackle earlier in the game. Graham Southernwood made the final pass for Plange to dive over in the corner taking two Trinity players with him. *Wakefield* claimed 'double movement' which the video appeared to up-hold, but referee Jim Smith gave the try and stood by his decision.

A rejuvenated *Hull* team roared to the top of the first division in dramatic style as they beat *Widnes* at The Boulevard. Both sides were unbeaten going into the tie and most expected it to be Hull that would crumble. Instead they put Widnes under pressure from the first minute with a brilliant performance from their pack, impressively lead by prop Andy Dannatt. The home side led 32-0 before Widnes found a reply with Davies carving an opening for Alan Tait to ease Widnes' embarrassment.

Bradford grabbed their first points of the season with a win at *Featherstone* in which the lead changed hands six times. *St Helens* seemed to have shrugged off their shaky start with a nine try defeat of *Hull Kingston Rovers*.

Warrington were on the receiving end of a good *Leeds* pack performance with costly signing John Gallagher getting his first try. *Wigan* made hard work of defeating relegation favourites *Rochdale* who restricted the home side with lots of tough tackling.

Halifax cruised to the top of the second division with a high scoring blitz on *Bramley*. *Carlisle* stayed in touch with an easy win over *Runcorn* who equalled Doncaster's record of 40 matches without a win. *Ryedale-York* registered a win over *Chorley* with a powerful seven try performance inspired by substitute Dean Williams.

Referee - Le best choice

Referee Alain Sablayrolles, one of France's top referees, was chosen to referee the forthcoming test matches between Great Britain and Australia.

Spartak Opener

A plan was announced for Soviet club Moscow Spartak to play a nine-a-side 30 minute game, against a London team as curtain raiser to the Great Britain-Australia test at Wembley. Spartak finished third in Russia's first ever knock-out tournament. The 24 strong Russian squad were also lined up to play an Aberavon amateur side and a Welsh select XIII.

Bateman Switch

Neath centre, Allan Bateman, became the latest Welsh Rugby Union player to switch codes when he signed a deal worth about £130,000 to join Warrington, bringing their spending in Wales to almost £400,000 in just three months.

Neath secretary, David Shaw, described Bateman's switch as a huge blow to Welsh Rugby Union and probably the biggest blow since Jonathan Davies went North. Bateman described the decision as the hardest that he had ever had to make.

Retirement

St Helens forward Paul Forber, 26, emotionally announced his retirement from Rugby League due to a serious neck injury. Paul had been determined to play-on despite advice to the contrary, until he was shown the x-rays and given a medical explanation. He had scored 42 tries in 191 games for Saints and was due a testimonial.

Teams of Month

Widnes and Salford were named as the Stones Bitter Teams of the month for August/September. Widnes for their victory in the Charity Shield plus wins over Wigan, Warrington, Bradford and Featherstone.

The second division prize went to Salford for victories over first division clubs Oldham and St Helens and by maintaining a 100% record in surging towards the top of their division.

Rugby League Euro MP's

Following the successful establishment of an All-party MPs' group at Westminster, the RFL and BARLA announced the formation of an inter-group of Euro-MPs with the aim of projecting Rugby League and protecting its interests within the European community.

September 29th - October 5th

RESULTS

LANCASHIRE CUP - FINAL

Salford 18	Widnes 24

DIVISION 1

Bradford 31	Wigan 30
Castleford 24	Featherstone 19
Hull KR 12	Wakefield 18
Leeds 23	St Helens 4
Rochdale 18	Hull 30
Sheffield 18	Warrington 20
Widnes 24	Oldham 10 mw

DIVISION 2

Carlisle 44	Bramley 15
Dewsbury 16	Fulham 6
Halifax 26	Ryedale-York 18
Keighley 14	Hunslet 44
Leigh 50	Chorley 4
Nottingham 27	Swinton 35
Runcorn 6	Huddersfield 19
Salford 21	Doncaster 4 mw
Trafford 32	Workington 8
Whitehaven 22	Barrow 15
Workington 8	Carlisle 13 mw

	P	Pts
Hull	4	8
Wakefield	4	6
Widnes	4	6
Wigan	4	5
Sheffield	4	5
Leeds	4	4
St Helens	4	4
Oldham	4	4
Warrington	4	4
Bradford	4	4
Hull KR	4	3
Castleford	4	2
Featherstone	4	1
Rochdale	4	0

	P	Pts
Carlisle	5	10
Halifax	5	8
Swinton	4	8
Whitehaven	5	8
Salford	4	8
Leigh	4	6
Ryedale-York	4	6
Trafford	4	6
Huddersfield	4	6
Hunslet	4	4
Doncaster	4	4
Workington	5	4
Fulham	4	2
Keighley	4	2

ROUNDUP

Salford came within a hair's breadth of defeating the favourites, *Widnes*, and lifting the Lancashire Cup. It took international winger Martin Offiah to grab the winning points for the Chemics just six minutes from time. When David Fell scored for Salford and Kerry kicked the conversion, it gave the second division outfit a six point lead and an upset looked on the cards. However, Widnes crashed back into the game with a try from David Smith after 68 minutes. Then came Offiah's try to seal the game for Widnes.

The game between *Bradford Northern* and *Wigan* produced some of the best Rugby League seen in many-a-year. There was also controversy after the half-time hooter had sounded. GB captain, Ellery Hanley, continued to press a point with referee Robin Whitfield who decided that enough was enough and told him to stay in the dressing room.

Castleford scored their first victory of the season despite a second-half comeback by *Featherstone* who had been losing 20-1. *Wakefield Trinity* also produced a comeback after trailing by 12-6 with just 10 minutes to go, to defeat a hapless *Hull KR* at Craven Park. *Leeds* handed out a sound defeat to *St Helens* with Garry Schofield having a triumphant return from injury. *Rochdale* gave league leaders *Hull* a real fright before going down to their fourth defeat. The *Warrington* pack proved just a bit too strong as they handed out the first defeat of the season to the *Sheffield Eagles*.

Carlisle took their time to get going, but when they did they ripped the *Bramley* defence apart, to go top of the Second Division. *Halifax* kept their early season run of good play going with a comfortable win over Yorkshire promotion rivals *Ryedale-York*.

Kangaroos Bounce in

The Australians arrived in Britain for their 13-match tour with their coach, Bobby Fulton, insisting that they were a stronger team than the 1982 & 1986 tourists.

Customs & Excise

A Customs and Excise petition to wind up Hunslet was dismissed in the High Court after the Registrar heard that Hunslet's VAT debt and costs had been paid in full.

GB Squad

The Great Britain squad for the first test against the Australians was announced as:

Davies (Widnes)	Schofield (Leeds)
Edwards (Wigan)	Dixon (Leeds)
Gibson (Leeds)	Fairbank (Bradford)
Gregory (Wigan)	Hanley (Wigan)
Hampson (Wigan)	Harrison (Hull)
Loughlin (St Helens)	Jackson (Hull)
Lydon (Wigan)	Platt (Wigan)
Offiah (Widnes)	Powell (Leeds)
Powell (Sheffield)	Ward (St Helens)
Betts (Wigan)	

Malcolm Reilly named six players who had not toured in the Winter tour of Papua New Guinea and New Zealand. Tourist prop Kelvin Skerrett was left out on fitness doubts. The coach also said that players not included in the squad could still push for a place.

Hanley Ban

GB captain, Ellery Hanley, received a two match ban following his dismissal at half-time in Wigan's game against Bradford Northern. Referee Robin Whitfield had dismissed Hanley for using 'foul and abusive' language. However, the ban was reduced to one game on appeal because it was Ellery's first dismissal. The reduction meant that Hanley would be able to take part in Wigan's game against the touring Australians, which he would have otherwise missed.

Keighley forward Mark Fairbank was less lucky, he received a ban for six games after being sent off against Hunslet, and team-mate Ricky Winterbottom also got a one match ban.

Back Already

St Helens forward Paul Forber was given the go-ahead by a specialist to make a comeback, only a week after having quit the game. The specialist thought the damage to his spine was not as serious as first thought.

October 6th - October 12th

RESULTS

TOURMATCHES

St Helens 4	Australia 34
Wakefield 18	Australia 36 mw

DIVISION 1

Bradford 12	Leeds 21
Featherstone 25	Sheffield 22
Hull 24	Wigan 4
Oldham 25	Hull KR 28
Warrington 26	Rochdale 9
Widnes 46	Castleford 4

	P	Pts
Hull	5	10
Widnes	5	8
Leeds	5	6
Wakefield	4	6
Warrington	5	6
Sheffield	5	5
Wigan	5	5
Hull KR	5	5
St Helens	4	4
Oldham	5	4
Bradford	5	4
Featherstone	5	3
Castleford	5	2
Rochdale	5	0

DIVISION 2

Barrow 12	Dewsbury 11
Batley 17	Nottingham 0
Chorley 4	Whitehaven 19
Doncaster 14	Keighley 11
Fulham 20	Bramley 6
Huddersfield 12	Trafford 28
Hunslet 52	Runcorn 12
Ryedale-York 12	Salford 19
Swinton 13	Halifax 20

	P	Pts
Carlisle	5	10
Halifax	6	10
Salford	5	10
Whitehaven	6	10
Trafford	5	8
Swinton	5	8
Hunslet	5	6
Leigh	4	6
Ryedale-York	5	6
Doncaster	5	6
Huddersfield	5	6
Fulham	5	4
Workington	5	4
Batley	4	2

ROUNDUP

The *Australians* fired the first warning shot of what might be to come, when they comprehensively beat *St Helens* at Knowsley Road. Mal Meninga, the Australian captain and ex-Saints player, opened and closed the try-scoring as the Kangaroos ran in eight tries. In a powerful performance, the tourists ran up a 30-0 lead inside 53 minutes and then seemed to coast along with a victory assured.

Hull underlined their challenge for the championship by defeating *Wigan* to stay at the top of the first division with a 100% record. In a game full of tension, the basis of the Hull victory came from their pack who dominated the Wigan six. Garry Schofield showed that he was back on form as *Leeds* cruised in three tries in the first 16 minutes to inflict defeat on *Bradford Northern* in the local derby.

    Rochdale Hornets continued to look for their first points, but went down again to *Warrington* at Wilderspool. *Hull KR's* celebrations at beating *Oldham* in a close game, were marred by the dismissal of David Bishop for a late tackle on Charlie McAllister. *Widnes* crushed *Castleford* in their Saturday game to go into second position in the division. Martin Pearson landed eight goals to give *Featherstone* their first victory of the season, over *Sheffield Eagles*.

Unbeaten *Salford* proved just a little too strong in the forwards for *Ryedale-York*. *Whitehaven* maintained their good start to the season with a victory over *Chorley* in a hard-fought match at Duke Street. *Hunslet* continued *Runcorn's* bad run with an easy win after only leading 20-12 at half-time. Greg Austin's speed helped *Halifax* come from behind to beat *Swinton* after the visitors had wasted several chances.

Bishop Controversy

At the start of the week, Oldham said that they were considering asking the RFL for a life ban on David Bishop after the Hull KR player was sent off for a dangerous tackle on Charlie McAllister. McAllister was still in hospital under observation with his cheekbone broken in three places and lucky, according to a specialist, to still have sight in his left eye. The RFL then placed a ban on Oldham commenting any further on the affair, in case they prejudiced the hearing. At the hearing the disciplinary committee decided that Bishop was not guilty of the charge.

Later in the week, Hull KR coach, Roger Millward, decided to drop Bishop from the team for the weekend's match. Bishop reacted by saying that he would never play for Hull KR again, so long as Millward was still coach. He also said that he was considering quitting the game and moving back to Wales.

Fulton Anger

Australian coach Bobby Fulton strongly criticised the referee after three of his mid-week players were dismissed during their victory over Wakefield. Referee Kevin Allatt had dismissed forward Mark Carroll and scrum-half Ricky Stuart for fighting, whilst David Gillespie was dismissed after the final hooter for swearing. Wakefield's John Thompson was also dismissed and two Australians plus one Wakefield player were sin-binned during the bad tempered game. The rather high penalty count in the game looked a little one sided. Australia were penalised 26 times whilst Wakefield were only penalised six times. Gillespie and Stuart were ruled to be 'not guilty' by the disciplinary committee.

Union Money

The Rugby Football Union met in Edinburgh to discuss their so-called amateur status. After a lengthy debate, the Union decided that players should be free to earn money by promoting goods, speaking at dinners, opening stores, etc. so long as money was not received as a benefit for playing rugby. That is to say, players became free to promote shoes, but not rugby boots.

Loughlin & Tait Out

Paul Loughlin of St Helens became the first player to be definitely ruled out of the first test against the Australians after ripping ankle tendons in training. Alan Tait, the Widnes full-back, also had to go into hospital for an operation on a groin injury which meant that he would miss all three tests.

BARLA postponements

BARLA gave permission for clubs to cancel their games on the 27th October to swell support for the first test at Wembley between Australia and Great Britain.

October 13th - October 19th

RESULTS

TOURMATCHES

Wigan 6	Australia 34
Cumbria 10	Australia 42 mw

DIVISION 1

Castleford 42	Wakefield 12
Warrington 2	Hull 3
Hull KR 22	Widnes 20
Leeds 16	Featherstone 18
Rochdale 19	Bradford 12
Sheffield 14	Oldham 24

DIVISION 2

Bramley 27	Chorley 18
Carlisle 17	Ryedale-York 17
Dewsbury 4	Swinton 18
Halifax 82	Runcorn 8
Huddersfield 10	Leigh 22
Keighley 22	Fulham 29
Nottingham 12	Workington 23
Salford 76	Barrow 10
Trafford 48	Hunslet 26
Whitehaven 6	Doncaster 9*
*(Later amended to 6-10)	

	P	Pts
Hull	6	12
Widnes	6	8
Hull KR	6	7
Leeds	6	6
Warrington	6	6
Oldham	6	6
Wakefield	5	6
Wigan	5	5
Sheffield	6	5
Featherstone	6	5
St Helens	4	4
Bradford	6	4
Castleford	6	4
Rochdale	6	2

	P	Pts
Halifax	7	12
Salford	6	12
Carlisle	6	11
Trafford	6	10
Swinton	6	10
Whitehaven	7	10
Leigh	5	8
Doncaster	6	8
Ryedale-York	6	7
Hunslet	6	6
Fulham	6	6
Huddersfield	6	6
Workington	6	6
Batley	4	2

ROUNDUP

Wigan's hopes of becoming the first British side to defeat the *Australians* since 1978, in a game that had been billed as the '4th Test', ended in a humiliating club-record defeat. In a game which bore remarkable similarities to their win over St Helens the previous week, the Kangaroos romped in seven tries and seemed to be 'cruising' at the end. The crowd of 25,101 fell silent after the first few minutes.

    Hull stayed at the top of the first division with a narrow victory over *Warrington* in the Saturday game, despite there being no tries the game was exciting to watch with plenty of open play. *Leeds* suffered another set-back when they lost to *Featherstone* at Headingley. Winger Alan Banks scored a try in injury time to level the scores and then youngster Martin Pearson scored the goal to get the points for Featherstone. *Hull KR* pulled themselves up into third position in the league with a win over *Widnes*, a happier end to a traumatic week.

    Rochdale provided the other upset of the day by beating a totally un-inspired *Bradford* side, the Hornets getting their first points of the season in a game full of mistakes by both sides. *Sheffield* fell to their third defeat in a row to two late *Oldham* tries. *Castleford* won their 'replay' of the Yorkshire Cup final against *Wakefield*, this time by a more convincing margin, thanks to good games from their half-backs Gary French and Graham Steadman.

In the second division, *Halifax* jumped to the top on points difference after running in 82 against hapless *Runcorn*. *Salford* also registered a big score as they maintained their 100% record by beating *Barrow*. *Carlisle* and *Ryedale-York* showed that the division could be close when they played out a tight draw.

Bishop Saga Continues

The Hull KR board met to discuss David Bishop's retort to being dropped for the game against Widnes. After initially saying that they wanted a 'cooling-off' period, they decided to transfer-list him for £120,000. The Chairman did, however, say that the door was open for reconciliation if Bishop wanted to return from Wales and apologise to Millward. Charlie McAllister had been consulting with solicitors with a view to suing Bishop for loss of earnings, but Oldham said that no action would be taken and that they would ensure that McAllister did not suffer a loss of earnings. Millward stated that he would be leaving Hull KR at the end of the season. He said that it was the hardest decision that he had ever had to make but he had been considering leaving before the whole Bishop affair started.

Life Ban

John Donohue, teenage scrum-half for Leigh, received a life ban after trial by video. The disciplinary committee decided that Donohue should be banned 'sine die' for a high tackle in an 'A' team game in which Mike Neale of Wigan received a fractured cheek-bone. An appeal was planned for November 2nd.

Demoted ?

League public relations officer, David Howes, declined to comment on reports that referee Robin Whitfield had been 'demoted' to second division games. Controller of referees Fred Lindop was in Russia on behalf of the League. However, Mr Whitfield said he would be seeking a meeting with Lindop as soon as he returned because he had not been awarded a first division game for four weeks. Mr Whitfield was the referee who gave GB captain Ellery Hanley his first sending off in the match against Bradford Northern.

Karen Replaced

Karen Almond was dropped as captain of the England ladies team for their first ever overseas international against Holland. Karen was replaced by Giselle Prangnell at fly half, but retained a spot on the subs bench.

Regal Trophy Anger

The draw was made for the preliminary and first round of the Regal Trophy. Leeds were drawn at home to Halifax and Sheffield at home to Bradford in the preliminary rounds, prompting complaints from Sheffield and Bradford. Eagles boss, Gary Hetherington, complained that they would have to postpone a lucrative game against Leeds to play in the preliminary round. Bradford Northern Chairman, Chris Caisley, said that he supported Hetherington's view as Bradford had lost a televised game against St Helens.

October 20th - October 26th

RESULTS

TOURMATCH

Leeds 10	Australia 22

DIVISION 1

Bradford 26	Hull KR 10
Featherstone 38	Rochdale 8
Hull 34	Sheffield 6
Oldham 4	Warrington 2
St Helens 16	Castleford 29
Wakefield 6	Widnes 16

	P	Pts
Hull	7	14
Widnes	7	10
Oldham	7	8
Featherstone	7	7
Hull KR	7	7
Leeds	6	6
Warrington	7	6
Bradford	7	6
Wakefield	6	6
Castleford	7	6
Wigan	5	5
Sheffield	7	5
St Helens	5	4
Rochdale	7	2

DIVISION 2

Barrow 26	Bramley 7
Batley 10	Trafford 2
Chorley 2	Salford 50
Doncaster 29	Huddersfield 20
Hunslet 19	Dewsbury 10
Leigh 56	Nottingham 6
Runcorn 12	Fulham 22
Ryedale-York 18	Halifax 16
Swinton 22	Carlisle 10
Workington 42	Keighley 0

	P	Pts
Salford	7	14
Halifax	8	12
Swinton	7	12
Carlisle	7	11
Leigh	6	10
Trafford	7	10
Doncaster	7	10
Whitehaven	7	10
Ryedale-York	7	9
Hunslet	7	8
Workington	7	8
Fulham	7	8
Huddersfield	7	6
Batley	5	4

ROUNDUP

Leeds offered the Test selectors a glimmer of hope as they held the *Australian* tourists for 50 minutes at Headingley. The Loiners led 10-6 at half time through enterprising play by Schofield and quick thinking by Gallagher. An upset was on the cards until 6'4" and 17 stone Paul Sironen pulled the Kangaroos back with two unstoppable runs to the line.

Sheffield's hopes against the league leaders were wrecked just before half time when *Hull* ran in three tries during a five minute spell, to go into the break with a 24-0 lead. Despite taking an early lead, *St Helens* suffered a home defeat as *Castleford* notched up their first away league win of the season. Castleford's Graham Steadman scored a hat-trick of tries and landed five goals plus a drop goal for a personal haul of 23 points. *Bradford's* Kiwi signing Darrall Shelford ran in a hat-trick of tries as the leagues' most inconsistent side notched up a victory over an uninterested *Hull KR*. All of Bradford's six tries were scored by Union converts; Gerald Cordle (2) and Neil Summers getting the other tries.

Another hat-trick was scored by Ian Smales for *Featherstone*, as the Rovers registered their third successive victory, this time against Rochdale. Smales had switched from the pack to centre when Newlove was ruled out with flu. *Wakefield* had no answer to the smart play of *Widnes'* Jonathan Davies. The Welsh convert grabbed the first points with a solo 90-yard run to the line, and saved a near certain try with a last minute tackle on Gary Price. *Oldham* emerged as victors against *Warrington,* Platt getting the edge for Oldham by kicking two penalties to Lyon's one.

Salford romped in another 50 points and promptly went to the top of the Second Division, with a win over *Chorley. Halifax* dropped to second position when they lost to *Ryedale-York* despite leading 2-16 just before half-time.

28

Squad Named

Jonathan Davies was the only surprise omission when the squad for the first test was named. The Widnes stand-off was omitted because of doubts about his step-father's health. Karl Harrison of Hull was the only un-capped player to be named. The line-up included five players from Wigan, and four from the Leeds side that played so well against the tourists at the week-end with Garry Schofield getting his desired place at stand-off.

The named squad was Hampson (Wigan), Eastwood (Hull), D Powell (Sheffield), Gibson (Leeds), Offiah (Widnes), Schofield (Leeds), Gregory (Wigan), Harrison (Hull), Jackson (Hull), Dixon (Leeds), R Powell (Leeds), Betts (Wigan), Hanley (Wigan). The substitutes were named as Hulme (Widnes), Fairbank (Bradford), Edwards (Wigan) and Ward (St Helens); with Irwin (Castleford) and Dannatt (Hull) as reserves.

Daley Out

The Australians suffered their first serious injury of the tour. Stand-off Laurie Daley was ruled out of the first test after breaking a bone in his hand at Headingley. He was replaced in the team by former Wallaby Rugby Union star Ricky Stuart.

Quarter Miler

Australia's Commonwealth Games gold medallist, Darren Clark, who called himself the world's fastest white quarter-miler, signed on a one year contract with Balmain.

Ticket Hopes

Ticket sales for the first test took a surge following Leeds' close game with the Kangaroos. David Howes said that they hoped to pass the best attendance figure of 50,583 set at Old Trafford on the previous Australian tour in 1986.

Hill's bookmakers gave Britain eight points start for the first Test, quoting both sides at 6-5 on. Australia were made 4-1 on favourites to win the Ashes series, with Britain at 11-4.

Challenge

A challenge was thrown down to Union officials in a bid to settle the argument about which code is the better. A Charity match was suggested to take the form of 40 minutes each code. A select team of Union players from the home countries would compete against a League team at Wembley or Twickenham with the proceeds going to the National Children's home.

Australian manager Keith Barnes was reported to have said that they could give the All Blacks a 30 point start.

October 27th - November 2nd

RESULTS

FIRST TEST

Great Britain 19   Australia 12

TOUR MATCH

Warrington 6   Australia 26 mw

DIVISION 1

Sheffield 16   Bradford 36 mw

DIVISION 2

Fulham 14   Batley 7
Hunslet 16   Leigh 24 mw
Salford 38   Trafford 12 mw

ROUNDUP

No games were scheduled for Sunday so that players and spectators could concentrate on the first test between Great Britain and the touring Kangaroos at Wembley. It is a good job because most people would have still been celebrating a memorable win for the Lions.

After 37 straight wins on British soil, and 160 points in just five games on this season's tour, most people did not give Great Britain much hope. However, the Lions upset the form book in front of a record crowd of 54,469 people.

Britain should have taken the lead as early as the 2nd minute when Paul Eastwood missed a 20m penalty for high tackling. However the Hull winger, who had been a controversial choice ahead of Jonathan Davies, did not prove to be the weak link. He scored two tries and a magnificent touchline penalty to make his personal haul of 14 points.

It was Ellery Hanley who showed the way, after a tense first half in which the forwards 'softened' one-another up. The loose-forward set off on one of his typical sinuous runs, beating the cover defence with a chip kick before passing to Daryll Powell. Powell then sent Eastwood in for his first try.

The Australians looked as if they could make their second half surge at any moment, though they did show an uncharacteristic lack of support for the man with the ball. When Mal Meninga did support the man, he easily ran over to bring the scores level at 6-6.

However, it was Hanley who made the next break-through, with a high kick. Australian full-back Gary Belcher fumbled the ball, which went loose, and Martin Offiah fell on it for a try.

Mark McGraw's solo run past four tackles for the Kangaroos second try was just an aberration in good British pressure. Garry Schofield wrapped things up for Britain when he chipped the defence and sent Eastwood in for his second try. Schofield also landed a drop-goal.

After the match, coach Bob Fulton said, "It had to happen sooner or later".

Sell Out

The RFL was swamped with requests for tickets for the remaining two tests at Old Trafford and Elland Road following Great Britain's victory in the first Test. As a result, all seats were sold out for both remaining tests (29,000 at Old Trafford and 18,000 at Elland Road) by the end of Monday. Officials, however, decided not to make the games all-ticket.

Talks Requested

Australian coach Bobby Fulton requested a meeting with the French referee Mr Sablayrolles. Fulton said that he wanted to clarify some points with Mr Sablayrolles after the first test, in particular the five-metre rule at the play-the-ball where the Australians were severally penalised in the first test.

Meninga Volunteers

Australian captain, Mal Meninga, volunteered to play in the mid-week game against Warrington. The rest of the team stayed as the usual 'mid-week' squad.

Five Axed

Five of the Australian players from the first test were axed from the team to play Castleford. Winger Michael Hancock, scrum-half Allan Langer, prop Martin Bella, hooker Kerrod Walters and second-row John Cartwright were the five to lose their places.

Merit Award

Maurice Oldroyd, the BARLA national administrator, won the League Writers' Association Merit Award for services to the game. Maurice was a founder member of BARLA when it started in 1973.

Castleford Fine

Castleford were fined £500 and ordered to pay £2,000 compensation to Granada TV, whose plans for screening the game live were badly hit by The Glassblowers' late arrival for their game against Widnes.

Ban Lifted

Leigh scrum-half, Jason Donohue, had his indefinite ban lifted by the Rugby League appeals committee, but was warned by his club and the League not to tackle dangerously in future. The hearing lasted 85 minutes and changed the suspension from 'sin die' to 12 matches.

November 3rd - November 9th

RESULTS

TOURMATCHES

Castleford 8	Australia 28
Halifax 18	Australia 36 mw

DIVISION 1

Bradford 25	Warrington 16
Hull KR 24	Featherstone 14
Rochdale 18	St Helens 30
Wakefield 22	Hull 6
Widnes 26	Leeds 8
Wigan 38	Oldham 15

	P	Pts
Hull	8	14
Widnes	8	12
Bradford	9	10
Hull KR	8	9
Wakefield	7	8
Oldham	8	8
Wigan	6	7
Featherstone	8	7
St Helens	6	6
Leeds	7	6
Warrington	8	6
Castleford	7	6
Sheffield	8	5
Rochdale	8	2

DIVISION 2

Carlisle 44	Barrow 26
Dewsbury 28	Doncaster 2
Halifax 28	Batley 3
Huddersfield 16	Workington 16
Keighley 32	Chorley 18
Nottingham 14	Ryedale-York 24
Runcorn 10	Hunslet 11
Salford 40	Bramley 0
Trafford 27	Fulham 28
Whitehaven 16	Swinton 24

	P	Pts
Salford	9	18
Halifax	9	14
Swinton	8	14
Carlisle	8	13
Leigh	7	12
Fulham	9	12
Ryedale-York	8	11
Doncaster	8	10
Trafford	9	10
Hunslet	9	10
Whitehaven	8	10
Workington	8	9
Huddersfield	8	7
Keighley	8	4

ROUNDUP

Australia kept their 100% record against club sides with a win over *Castleford* on Sunday, and a mid-week win over second division *Halifax*. The tourists again gave away a lot of penalties, losing them 17-7 against Castleford.

Wakefield provided the upset by dishing out the first defeat of the season to *Hull* at Belle Vue. David Topliss chose a team to take the game down the middle to Hull and it paid off. *Widnes* stayed in second position with a comfortable win over a *Leeds* side short on ideas in the Saturday game. *Hull KR* beat *Featherstone* at Craven Park with most of the points coming from mistakes.
     Bradford scored a good win over *Warrington* when Paul Medley turned the tide in Bradford's favour with a 75 yard individual try. George Mann helped stop *St Helens* slide down the table with a strong performance in their win over bottom of the table *Rochdale*. *Wigan* proved too strong for *Oldham* with Andy Gregory calling most of the shots.

Runcorn came as close as they could to stopping their record breaking run of bad results when they went down by just one point to *Hunslet*. *Ryedale-York* kept in touch with the leaders with an away win over *Nottingham*. *Salford* continued their untroubled run with an easy win over *Bramley*. *Halifax* stayed in second position with a win over *Batley*. *Swinton* survived a last minute comeback to beat *Whitehaven*. *Carlisle* leapfrogged over Leigh into fourth position with a home win over *Barrow*.

Loughlin and Platt Return

Paul Loughlin and Andy Platt were named in the 19 man training squad for the second test against Australia, dropping Shaun Irwin and Andy Dannatt. Loughlin had been forced out of the first test squad with ankle ligament trouble and Platt had missed the squad with a knee injury.

Platt was later named in the starting line-up, whilst Loughlin was named as one of the four substitutes. Shaun Edwards and Karl Fairbank were relegated from the substitutes bench to travelling reserves.

£1,000,000

Great Britain's win in the first test, and record match attendances allowed the Rugby League to top the one million pound mark for the three match test series. The Police insisted that the third test at Elland Road be made an all-ticket game, and the remaining 14,000 standing places were sold out within days of going on sale.

Unbeaten Runs

Unbeaten runs through October by Hull and Fulham earned them the Stones Bitter 'Team of the Month' awards. Hull beat Wigan, Sheffield and Warrington to win their £500, whilst Fulham collected £350 for averaging 20 points per game in wins over Bramley, Batley, Keighley and Runcorn.

Hetherington Reprimanded

Sheffield Eagles boss Gary Hetherington was reprimanded by the League following newspaper comments that it was 'ridiculous' to give the Regal Trophy Preliminary round tie against Bradford preference over the scheduled league game against Leeds.

Hetherington apologised to the board for his comments, and accepted that the game had the full machinery necessary for a debate on the subject to be heard without recourse to newspapers.

Charlton Re-instated

Whitehaven forward, Gary Charlton, became the second player to be reinstated from a life ban in as many weeks. Charlton who had not played for 11 months following an incident in which Castleford's Graham Steadman received a broken nose and fractured cheekbone, was told that he could play from 1st December.

Charlton had been training with Carlisle for some weeks, but Whitehaven maintained that he was still their player and a League inquiry was judged to be necessary to see where his playing future would resume.

November 10th - November 16th

RESULTS

SECOND TEST

Great Britain 10   Australia 14

TOUR MATCH

Hull   4   Australia 34 mw

DIVISION 1

Featherstone 6	Castleford 22
Hull KR 6	Wigan 36 mw
Leeds 64	Rochdale 4
Oldham 16	Bradford 18
St Helens 34	Sheffield 17
Warrington 10	Wakefield 18

REGAL TROPHY- Preliminary round

Doncaster 14   Ryedale-York 12 mw

DIVISION 2

Barrow 12	Huddersfield 26
Batley 26	Whitehaven 16
Bramley 44	Runcorn 6
Chorley 38	Nottingham 19
Doncaster 19	Trafford 14
Fulham 4	Ryedale-York 9
Hunslet 6	Keighley 14
Leigh 24	Carlisle 16
Swinton 13	Dewsbury 6
Workington 24	Halifax 16

	P	Pts
Hull	8	14
Widnes	8	12
Bradford	10	12
Wakefield	8	10
Hull KR	9	9
Wigan	7	9
Leeds	8	8
St Helens	7	8
Oldham	9	8
Castleford	8	8
Featherstone	9	7
Warrington	9	6
Sheffield	9	5
Rochdale	9	2

	P	Pts
Salford	9	18
Swinton	9	16
Halifax	10	14
Leigh	8	14
Carlisle	9	13
Ryedale-York	9	13
Fulham	10	12
Doncaster	9	12
Workington	9	11
Trafford	10	10
Hunslet	10	10
Whitehaven	9	10
Huddersfield	9	9
Batley	8	6

ROUNDUP

Hull, Hull KR, Wigan and Widnes did not play due to players being on test duty. *Leeds,* despite having had four players on test duty, took apart *Rochdale* with 11 tries, but Garry Schofield picked up a minor injury. *Castleford* won their third successive game in a one sided match at Post Office Road to beat *Featherstone* with half-backs Steadman and French leading the way.

Bradford also continued their recent good form to score their fourth successive win in a close game at *Oldham* which saw the Bradford line under a lot of pressure in the last five minutes. *St Helens* scored a bizarre try from a ball headed forward to set up a victory over *Sheffield*. *Wakefield* recorded their first victory at Wilderspool for 13 years as *Warrington* slumped to their 5th straight defeat.

Halifax's hopes for promotion took another set-back when they lost to *Workington* after having a prop sent off before half-time. *Swinton* took advantage and jumped over Halifax into second position with a home victory over *Dewsbury*.

Ryedale-York got the better of a tight game at *Fulham* with two penalties and a drop goal in the last 10 minutes. The TV cameras turned up at *Bramley* in the hope of seeing an upset, but they only served to inspire the home side to keep up *Runcorn's* run of defeats.

SECOND TEST

Australia levelled the test series with a last minute try in the second test at a packed Old Trafford. The crowd of 46,615 were thrilled by another close and exciting game, the result of which was in doubt until the final hooter went.

The tourists had made eight changes from the team that took the field at Wembley, the most telling of which was the inclusion of Benny Elias at hooker. Elias never stopped working and produced more than a few good runs to deservedly get the man-of-the-match award. Great Britain tried hard but they never quite regained the commitment and ingenuity they showed at Wembley. They rarely put Australia under sustained pressure.

It was Australia who opened the scoring with a try by Dale Shearer from long distance, but Great Britain hit back with a penalty which was landed by Paul Eastwood, for the only scores in the first half. After 52 minutes Paul Dixon charged over the line in a repeat of a move that he had produced in the first half. However, this time the Kangaroos failed to hold him on his back and Dixon touched down. Only four minutes later a typical Australian passing movement, involving 12 passes, had the British defence in disarray before Andrew Ettingshausen kicked from the wing for Cliff Lyons to score. For once, captain Mal Meninga managed to convert.

Martin Offiah injured his knee in a tackle which brought on Paul Loughlin who had missed the first test. Any thoughts that he lacked speed were dispelled when he intercepted a pass from Stuart to race 50 yards for a try to put the scores level at 10-10. Eastwood again missed the kick, and after being the hero of Wembley, he was reported to be inconsolable in the changing rooms.

With good British pressure near the end, it looked as if the game was heading for a draw and Great Britain were going to avoid losing the Ashes. Then, with only 20 seconds on the clock, Australia struck from their own 25 yard area. Ricky Stuart took the ball for 70 yards after avoiding Lee Jackson, Mal Meninga was in support to receive the ball and to score the match winning try.

Wigan Compensation

Wigan said that they were starting legal action against Australian club Western Suburbs following non-payment of a compensation demand over Ellery Hanley. Hanley had returned from a guest spell at the Australian club in the summer with a pelvic injury which kept him out of the Wigan squad until December.

More Sponsorship

British Nuclear Fuels announced that they would be sponsoring both the senior and the youth BARLA teams in their three match test series against France for an undisclosed but "substantial" sum.

Not Worth the Pay ?

Halifax players donated the pay they earned in their defeat at Workington to charity. The suggestion came from coach Peter Roe who was reportedly angry and upset at what he called the teams' "unprofessional" approach.

McAllister Back

Oldham's Charlie McAllister returned to Rugby League action in a reserve's match after being given the all clear to play again from a specialist. His return came just six weeks after his cheekbone was shattered in four places by a tackle from Hull KR's David Bishop.

35

November 17th - November 23rd

RESULTS

REGAL TROPHY PRELIMINARY ROUND

Dudley Hill 18	Dewsbury 24
Saddleworth 35	Egremont 18
Carlisle 10	Wakefield 28
Leeds 58	Halifax 6
Sheffield 8	Bradford 12

DIVISION 1

Bradford 18	St Helens 16 mw
Castleford 28	Oldham 10
Hull 17	Warrington 8
Rochdale 18	Hull KR 32
Wigan 24	Featherstone 4

	P	Pts
Hull	9	16
Bradford	11	14
Widnes	8	12
Wigan	8	11
Hull KR	10	11
Wakefield	8	10
Castleford	9	10
Leeds	8	8
St Helens	8	8
Oldham	10	8
Featherstone	10	7
Warrington	10	6
Sheffield	9	5
Rochdale	10	2

TOUR MATCH

Widnes 10	Australia 15

DIVISION 2

Barrow 10	Trafford 6
Halifax 42	Bramley 12 mw
Keighley 18	Doncaster 10
Nottingham 14	Leigh 52
Runcorn 6	Salford 26
Ryedale-York 22	Workington 0
Swinton 13	Fulham 4
Whitehaven 12	Hunslet 7

	P	Pts
Salford	10	20
Swinton	10	18
Leigh	9	16
Halifax	11	16
Ryedale-York	10	15
Carlisle	9	13
Whitehaven	10	12
Fulham	11	12
Doncaster	10	12
Workington	10	11
Hunslet	11	10
Trafford	11	10
Huddersfield	9	9
Keighley	10	8

ROUNDUP

Australia completed their games against the British club sides with their 100% record intact after they were made to fight at *Widnes*. *Castleford* showed that only 12 players were needed to beat an injury hit *Oldham* despite Charlie McAllister's return. *Hull* got the better of a tight game against *Warrington* to stay at the top of Division One and to put the Wire into the relegation zone. *Rochdale* fell to another defeat, this time at the hands of *Hull KR* to stay firmly anchored at the bottom.

Leeds ran rampant in the Regal Trophy preliminary round over a *Halifax* side that showed no resemblance to the one which made the final last year. *Sheffield* fell to their third defeat of the season at the hands of *Bradford* despite giving Northern a close run in the final 10 minutes. *Carlisle* also dropped out of the trophy to a solid but unexciting *Wakefield*.

Leaders *Salford* could only manage 28 points against bottom side *Runcorn* in the Second Division giving Highfield the hope of some points this season. *Swinton* kept the pressure on Salford with a win in the capital over *Fulham*. *Ryedale-York* managed to shut out *Workington* to serve notice that they were also in with a promotion shout as the division started to take shape.

Whinging Aussies

Australian coach Bobby Fulton, who had been whinging about a lot of things on the tour, continued to beat the 'Whinging Poms' into second place with an attack on Widnes. This time Fulton claimed that the Widnes players had been trying to gouge his players eyes. His claims had some form of substance because giant forward Paul Sironen had to retire from the game with a scratched eyeball to become doubtful for the third test.

New Chairman

Rochdale Hornets chose former Swinton second row forward, Dick Bonser, to be their new Chairman in succession to Len Stansfield, with John Nicholson at Vice-Chairman. The Hornets also decided not to go ahead with the signing of St Helens forward David Lever who had been on loan at Spotland.

Jones Out of Contention

Mark Jones, the former Welsh Rugby Union international, fell out of contention for a place in the Hull side for the next couple of games with a recurrence of ankle ligament problems. Jones' injury problems added his name to a long list of players who have suffered from injury problems after switching codes.

Reilly Faithful

Coach Malcolm Reilly stayed faithful to the line-up which faced the Australians in the second test. Despite strong speculation to the contrary, he picked the same team to take to the pitch in the third and final test at Elland Road.

The only changes in the squad were Jonathan Davies and Mike Gregory being brought onto the substitutes bench in place of Paul Loughlin and Kevin Ward.

Ticket Claims

The secretary of the unofficial supporters association issued a press release, saying that it was scandalous that corporate hospitality packages were still available when ordinary fans could not get a ticket to the final test.

However, the claim that one London based agency had hundreds of tickets still available was dismissed by RL public affairs official David Howes, who indicated that the London company had bought 10 tickets and 5 remained unsold.

Meanwhile, Leeds police appealed to fans without a ticket to stay away from Elland Road and for those fans with tickets to turn up early so as to help avoid congesting the area.

November 24th - November 30th

RESULTS

TESTMATCH

Great Britain 0	Australia 14

DIVISION 1

Featherstone 14	Hull 6
Hull KR 12	Bradford 4
Leeds 41	Castleford 12 mw
Oldham 14	Widnes 24
St Helens 44	Rochdale 14
Wakefield 14	Wigan 12 mw
Warrington 30	Sheffield 8

	P	Pts
Hull	10	16
Widnes	9	14
Bradford	12	14
Hull KR	11	13
Wakefield	9	12
Wigan	9	11
St Helens	9	10
Castleford	10	10
Leeds	9	10
Featherstone	11	9
Warrington	11	8
Oldham	11	8
Sheffield	10	5
Rochdale	11	2

REGAL TROPHY - 1st round

Rochdale 30	Saddleworth 10 mw

DIVISION 2

Barrow 18	Halifax 46
Batley 14	Ryedale-York 26
Chorley 8	Carlisle 12
Fulham 14	Dewsbury 10
Huddersfield 17	Runcorn 14
Hunslet 22	Doncaster 10
Leigh 12	Swinton 20
Nottingham 24	Bramley 21
Salford 40	Whitehaven 6
Workington 36	Trafford 6

	P	Pts
Salford	11	22
Swinton	11	20
Halifax	12	18
Ryedale-York	11	17
Leigh	10	16
Carlisle	10	15
Fulham	12	14
Workington	11	13
Hunslet	12	12
Doncaster	11	12
Whitehaven	11	12
Huddersfield	10	11
Trafford	12	10
Keighley	10	8

ROUNDUP

Featherstone surprised leaders *Hull* at Post Office Road thanks to goalkicking substitute Martin Pearson; the 19 year old scored one try, set up another and landed two goals. *Hull KR* made the best of a hard fought match to come back against *Bradford*, Bryan Neibling and Paul Lyman got the Robin's tries. Jonathan Davies bounced back from the test defeat to score two tries and land two goals in *Widnes's* win at *Oldham*.

    Rochdale suffered a second half collapse after trailing only 2-4 at half time as *St Helens* ran in three tries in six minutes just after the re-start and then added another four. *Warrington* ended their run of six defeats at the expense of *Sheffield* whose own losing run extended to eight matches, and Allan Bateman got his first try in Rugby League. *Wigan* fell to only their second defeat of the season at *Wakefield* thanks to a try from Ged Byrne, a former *Wigan* player. *Leeds* ran riot over *Castleford* to bring their points total to 163 in their last three games.

Nottingham recorded their first win of the season against *Bramley*, a trialist winger getting one of city's tries. Stand-off David Fell scored a hat-trick as *Salford* easily beat *Whitehaven* to stay top of the division. *Barrow* led *Halifax* by 12-0 after 34 minutes, but 'fax hit back to win thanks to debut player Jimmy Irvine recently signed from Hull KR. *Swinton* got their first victory at *Leigh* for 23 years in a game delayed 25 minutes because of floodlight failure.

Lions Yield to Roos

The fate of the ashes was finally decided in Australia's favour when they won the third and final test at Elland Road to clinch the series 2-1 and to leave Great Britain pondering 'what might have been'.

A mistake by Wembley hero Garry Schofield indirectly led to the first Australian try. The stand-off badly fumbled a pass and centre Carl Gibson injured his shoulder recovering the situation. While Great Britain were temporarily down to 12 men, the tourist's scrum-half Ricky Stuart took full advantage and launched a huge 30 yard pass to cut out the British cover and to send Andrew Ettingshausen sliding over for the first try after only eight minutes.

Australia's tackling was very fierce, particularly on captain Ellery Hanley, but Britain also lacked ideas and seemed to be overcome by the occasion plus the pressure on them to win The Ashes. Even the other half-back hero of Wembley, Andy Gregory, couldn't get the team going and often seemed to be playing different moves to the rest of the backs.

Nevertheless, Britain kept Australia out for the rest of the first half and went in trailing only 0-4. Fitness was always going to tell in the wet and muddy conditions and in such a fiercely contested match.

And so it was that the inevitable happened. After only 12 minutes of the second half, another long pass by Stuart pulled Schofield out of the line to attempt the interception. Instead, the Aussie stand-off Cliff Lyons gathered the ball and sent his captain Mal Meninga in for the second try, making it a try in each test for the big centre.

The Ashes were secured with eight minutes to go following a break by Laurie Daley which was stopped by Jonathan Davies, only for Benny Elias to touchdown from a Steve Roach pass.

Warning to Rugby league

The second division clubs held a meeting to discuss player's contract payments. They then issued a warning to the League that many second division clubs might not be able to cope with the increasing size of contracts. Some of the clubs thought that player's contracts should be abolished, others thought that a 'capping' system similar to the Australian system should be introduced.

Bust-up

St Helens coach Mike McLennan and stand-off Tony Frodsham were disciplined by the club after a 'bust-up' between the two at a testimonial function for former British forward Roy Haggarty.

Long Serving Departure

Forward Keith Bell, 36, ended his 19 year spell at Featherstone when he joined Hunslet on a free transfer. Bell joined Featherstone from junior rugby in 1971 and he made 417 first team appearances.

Murphy Money Row

Alex Murphy was ordered to appear before Leigh's board of directors after criticising them in public. Murphy had accused the Leigh board of breaking their promises to him of money that he needed to build a side capable of winning promotion back to the First Division.

December 1st - December 7th

RESULTS

REGAL TROPHY - 1st round

Barrow 16	Featherstone 54	Oldham 26	Salford 6
Bradford 12	Workington 11	Swinton 7	St Helens 31
Bramley 30	Dewsbury 16	Trafford 10	Doncaster 10
Fulham 8	Castleford 14	(Doncaster 17	Trafford 7) mw
Huddersfield 13	Keighley 15	Wakefield 40	Hunslet 8
Leeds 26	Hull KR 22	Warrington 33	Runcorn 7
Leigh 66	Chorley 5	Whitehaven 6	Wigan 24
Nottingham 4	Batley 35	Widnes 26	Hull 16

ROUNDUP

There were a few close escapes. The closest was at *Bradford* where *Workington* took the lead five minutes from the end with a drop goal, only to give away a penalty two minutes later for Northern's stand-in kicker and captain John Pendlebury to clinch the tie. *Wigan* failed to make the most of *Whitehaven's* lack of pace but scored 12 points in the last three minutes. *Castleford* just scraped a victory in London, with a late *Fulham* 'try' being disallowed for a double movement.

Jonathan Davies was again the inspiration of *Widnes* in an exciting match which saw the Chemics put on the rack by a fighting *Hull* side. *Hull KR* were the only First Division side to exit the Trophy thanks to a 70th minute try by *Leeds'* Garry Schofield. *St Helens* recovered from an early *Swinton* try to run in five for themselves. *Warrington* also grabbed five tries after leading lowly *Runcorn* just 6-1 at half-time.

Winger Martin Pearson put *Featherstone Rovers* on the score board after only five minutes with the first of Rovers' 10 tries against *Barrow*. *Leigh* scored more tries than *Chorley* had players left on the pitch as they ran in 12 tries and the visitor's had two players sent off. *Wakefield* also had Nick de Toit sent off for butting in *Trinity's* easy win over Hunslet.

The only draw was at *Trafford Borough* where the home side fought back to level the scores in the 72nd minute against *Doncaster*, only to lose the replay. *Oldham* avenged their defeat by *Salford* in the Lancashire Cup thanks to their props John Fairbank and Austin Donegan. *Bramley* proved to be stronger finishers than *Dewsbury* after the scores had been level 16-16 after 60 minutes.

Batley took 34 minutes to score their first try but dominated the second half to put *Nottingham* out in the first round once again. *Keighley* snatched victory four minutes from time in a nail-biting victory at *Huddersfield*, with the home side missing a last minute penalty in a 'kickable' position.

Gregory Retires

Great Britain scrum-half Andy Gregory, who played in all three tests against the Australians, announced his retirement from the International game. Gregory, aged 29, gained his first cap in 1981 and had made two tours down-under. The scrum-half said that he wanted to retire from the National squad so that the selectors would be able to groom a successor in time for the 1992 tour to Australia. Maurice Lindsay, the Great Britain manager, said that Gregory could be thought of as one of the most outstanding half-backs that had played Rugby League.

Lost Money

Warrington announced a loss of £34,000 for the season 1989/90 despite getting to the Challenge Cup final at Wembley. The deficit was down on the previous 12 month's loss of £76,000 but still added to the club's total liabilities which reached £680,000. Shareholders in the club were warned that the clearance of the liabilities remained a "difficult task". One of the main reasons for the deficit was a massive leap in wage payments which were up from £343,000 to £541,000.

St Helens announced a loss of £37,000, but this was compared to a profit of £69,000 in the previous 12 months.

Murphy to Stay

It was announced that Alex Murphy would stay on as coach to Leigh after his appearance in front of the Leigh board following allegations of defamatory comments he had made about them. The internal discussions were described as full and frank, and it was said that the air had been cleared. Murphy added that he felt sorry for the Leigh fans because the team needed strengthening, but there was no money available.

Drop Goal Awarded

Doncaster half-back Dean Carroll was officially credited with a drop goal nearly two months after kicking it. Carroll had his drop goal disallowed against Whitehaven when he kicked it after the hooter system had failed but before the referee had time to blow his whistle. The RFL's board of directors confirmed that the goal should have stood and that the result amended to Whitehaven 6 Doncaster 10 (from 6-9).

TV Row

A small row developed between the RFL and Widnes following The Chemics being named as a Saturday game for live BBC TV coverage (versus Hull and Leeds) for the second successive week. Widnes representatives said that the club was being overexposed and that they were losing out on larger gates. The RFL replied that they tried to spread the TV coverage around the clubs, but that Widnes should remember the BBC was the top TV contract and that it provided a showcase for the game. A compromise was reached and Widnes were awarded an extra £6,000 in compensation.

It was also decided that the starting time for the Challenge Cup final at Wembley should be brought forward to 2:30pm from 3:00pm to allow full, in-depth, post match coverage by TV.

Teams of the Month

Wakefield and Swinton won the divisional teams of the month awards after unbeaten runs in the league. Wakefield's run included a win over Wigan.

December 8th - December 14th

RESULTS

REGAL TROPHY - 2nd Round

Batley 20	Oldham 16
Bradford 28	Bramley 0 mw
Doncaster 10	Rochdale 14 mw
Featherstone 16	St Helens 33 mw
Wakefield 4	Castleford 20
Warrington 11	Leigh 6
Widnes 22	Leeds 6
Wigan 36	Keighley 16

DIVISION 2

Barrow 8	Ryedale-York 31
Carlisle 12	Dewsbury 10

ROUNDUP

The main concern of the week-end's games was the snow storms that were sweeping the country, causing the postponement of Bradford v Bramley, Doncaster v Rochdale and Featherstone v St Helens until mid-week.

Leeds were the first team out of the second round when they lost to *Widnes* in their game played on Saturday. The Loiners scored in the fifth minute against the wind, through Phil Ford. Strong defence kept the home side pointless until half-time. However a try within minutes of the re-start seemed to dent the visitor's confidence and Widnes took full advantage with Tony Myler outstanding at stand-off.

Second division *Batley* caused the upset of the round by coming back from 4-10 down at half-time to defeat first division *Oldham*. Batley's player coach Keith Rayne scored a hat-trick of tries, with the third try and winning points coming in the last minute of the game.

Warrington struggled into the next round in an unconvincing win over *Leigh* with second rower Bob Jackson taking the man-of-the-match.

Wigan predictably overcame second division *Keighley* despite the visitors scoring three tries. The holder's victory was ensured by a hat-trick of tries from centre Kevin Iro in a 10 minute spell during the first half hour.

Castleford raced to a 12-0 lead inside the first six minutes against *Wakefield* in their third meeting of the season. The visitors then ground down the Trinity defence in a game hampered by mud and snow.

When the snow was cleared; *Bradford's* defence looked impermeable as they swept aside *Bramley* on Tuesday night in a muddy encounter at Odsal and *St Helens* also progressed at the expense of *Featherstone*. The next evening *Doncaster* fought hard, but finally fell to two tries from *Rochdale's* hooker Martin Hall.

In the second division; *York* kept on the promotion trail with a hat-trick from Basil Ake and 22 points in the last quarter of an hour of the match, to defeat *Barrow*. *Dewsbury* came close to surprising *Carlisle* in their first match since Maurice Bamford was sacked, coming back against Carlisle's 12-0 lead.

Referees Summonsed

Robin Whitfield and Ray Tennant were ordered to appear before the RL board of directors, to explain their comments to newspapers, following Whitfield's demotion from the top 10 referees and Tennant's withdrawal from November's Wigan-Oldham league meeting.

Oldham Complaint

Oldham made a complaint about Batley's handling of their second round Regal Trophy game which included the sending off of loose forward John Cogger for "inciting" the crowd. The incident was said to involve one of Batley's female stewards grabbing Cogger's hair when Oldham's Paul Round scored a try. Cogger was then sent off for turning round and making a two-fingered gesture to the crowd. Oldham also said that they were treated dreadfully by the Second Division club, with even the ball boys swearing at the Oldham players.

Oldham thought that Cogger would be 'excused' despite police complaints, but the Disciplinary Committee saw it differently and gave the forward a two match suspension.

Barrow Comeback

Steve Norton, the 39 year old Barrow coach, said that he was going to make a playing comeback to help the struggling club. He expected to start playing for the first team in the new year

Scarborough Application

Scarborough were given a warm welcome with their plans for forming a new professional club at the ground of Scarborough FC. After an outline of their plans was given to the RL board of directors, they announced that a committee would look in to the proposals and a final decision would be made at the RL council members' meeting on January 9th.

Contract Dispute

Leigh's New Zealand test forward, Peter Ropati, was put on the transfer-list after continuing a dispute over his contract with the club. He joined David Ruane, Paul Topping and Andy Collier on the list at Hilton Park.

Virtual Sell Out

The RL announced a virtual sell out of the Challenge Cup Final at Wembley on April 27th 1991. David Howes said that it was the fastest ever 'sell-out' of The Final and they anticipated record takings of over £1.5 million. The 'sell-out' was of the 50,000 'spare' tickets, whilst 30,000 were reserved for the two clubs that would be competing.

Warrington Blow

Mike Gregory, the Warrington captain, was told that he had not only ruptured ligaments in his knee during the Regal Trophy game against Runcorn, but that he had also torn a cartilage. He expected to be out of action for the rest of the season.

December 15th - December 21st

RESULTS

REGAL TROPHY - 3rd Round

Castleford 14	Rochdale 19
Warrington 18	St Helens 12
Widnes 56	Batley 6
Wigan 6	Bradford 12

DIVISION 1

Castleford 22	Warrington 18 mw
Hull 31	Oldham 4
Sheffield 6	Leeds 24
Widnes 28	Hull KR 8 mw

DIVISION 2

Carlisle 19	Leigh 16
Dewsbury 7	Workington 5
Doncaster 0	Fulham 4
Halifax 38	Chorley 10
Keighley 38	Nottingham 6
Runcorn 12	Bramley 13
Ryedale-York 6	Huddersfield 7
Swinton 22	Hunslet 10
Trafford 20	Batley 8 mw
Whitehaven 12	Salford 38

	P	Pts
Hull	11	18
Widnes	10	16
Bradford	12	14
Hull KR	12	13
Leeds	10	12
Wakefield	9	12
Castleford	11	12
Wigan	9	11
St Helens	9	10
Featherstone	11	9
Warrington	12	8
Oldham	12	8
Sheffield	11	5
Rochdale	11	2

	P	Pts
Salford	12	24
Swinton	12	22
Halifax	13	20
Carlisle	12	19
Ryedale-York	13	19
Leigh	11	16
Fulham	13	16
Workington	12	13
Huddersfield	11	13
Hunslet	13	12
Doncaster	12	12
Whitehaven	12	12
Trafford	13	12
Keighley	11	10

ROUNDUP

The Regal Trophy quarter finals produced two surprises; *Bradford* travelled to Central Park and made *Wigan* look very ordinary with a solid defence that did not allow the holders to run the ball. *Castleford* maintained their reputation for inconsistency by falling to *Rochdale* despite the 22 point victory predicted by the handicap coupon. *Warrington* also progressed with a try five minutes from time by full-back Dave Lyon, to beat *St Helens*. *Widnes* predictably outclassed *Batley* with 11 tries, four of them by Martin Offiah.

In the first division; The floodlights failed for 12 minutes at the Don Valley Stadium and *Sheffield* failed to take advantage of a *Leeds* team reduced to 12 men when Simon Irving was sent off for tripping. *Oldham* did well to hold league leaders *Hull* to a two point lead at half-time but then folded to let in 25 points in the second half.

In the second division; There were three victories by just one point, a dour struggle at *Dewsbury* saw the home side pip *Workington*, *Huddersfield* struck a blow to *Ryedale-York*'s promotion hopes with a drop goal two minutes from time and *Runcorn* came within a hairs breadth of their first league point against *Bramley*. At the top, *Salford* and *Whitehaven* both picked up injuries as the leaders won easily. *Hunslet* lost to *Swinton* in the first 20 minutes when they let in 16 points. *Carlisle* jumped over *Leigh* in the league despite a barrage from the visiting side.

44

Christmas Goodwill

Trafford Borough chairman Mike Marsland announced that visiting fans would only be charged half-price entry to their mid-week game against Batley as a goodwill gesture for the festive season.
    Trafford were not so benevolent on the pitch and registered a glum win over the visitors to bring to an end their run of eight games without a win.

Warrington Extend List Further

Warrington added Great Britain under-21 stand-off Robert Turner to their transfer list at his own request. Although Turner had been the Wire's top scorer with 182 in the previous season, he had lost his place to Australian Chris O'Sullivan.

Seeding Call

Amateur Rugby League official Maurice Oldroyd made a renewed call for the first round of the Challenge Cup to be seeded, so that top teams would not face one another and so that amateur clubs would stand a chance of having a financially lucrative tie against a First Division club.

The draw was made, without seeding, for the preliminary and first rounds of the Challenge Cup, with Castleford and Wigan being drawn together in the first round. Leigh East got the most lucrative draw of the amateur clubs with a visit from Bradford Northern in the preliminary round.

Pulled out a Plum

Oldham's forward John Fairbank had an operation to have a pin inserted in a broken thumb, putting him out of action for two months.

Extra Time

The RFL announced that extra time would be played, for the first time, if the scores finished level in either of the two Regal Trophy semi-finals, to avoid fixture congestion during the festive period. If the scores remained level after extra-time then the two teams would have to return the next day for a replay at the same venue. (Bradford Northern v Rochdale and Warrington v Widnes were the two semi-final draws).

Reprimand

Referee Ray Tennant was given a severe reprimand by the League's board of directors for the manner in which he turned down three match appointments.

December 22nd - December 28th

RESULTS

REGAL TROPHY - semi final

Bradford 13	Rochdale 2

DIVISION 1

Featherstone 14	Wakefield 8 bh
Hull 22	Castleford 6 bh
Leeds 26	Bradford 8 bh
Oldham 18	Rochdale 13 bh
Sheffield 18	St Helens 8
St Helens 15	Wigan 28 bh
Warrington 2	Widnes 6 bh
Wigan 22	Leeds 16

	P	Pts
Hull	12	20
Widnes	11	18
Wigan	11	15
Leeds	12	14
Bradford	13	14
Hull KR	12	13
Wakefield	10	12
Castleford	12	12
Featherstone	12	11
St Helens	11	10
Oldham	13	10
Warrington	13	8
Sheffield	12	7
Rochdale	12	2

DIVISION 2

Barrow 34	Carlisle 4 bh
Batley 9	Carlisle 38
Bramley 12	Doncaster 14
Chorley 10	Keighley 14
Dewsbury 6	Batley 4 bh
Doncaster 4	Ryedale-York 11 bh
Huddersfield 52	Whitehaven 18
Huddersfield 20	Chorley 6 bh
Keighley 6	Halifax 12 bh
Leigh 40	Barrow 4
Nottingham 6	Dewsbury 38
Ryedale-York 34	Runcorn 0
Workington 22	Hunslet 12

	P	Pts
Salford	12	24
Ryedale-York	15	23
Halifax	14	22
Swinton	12	22
Carlisle	14	21
Leigh	12	18
Huddersfield	13	17
Fulham	13	16
Workington	13	15
Doncaster	14	14
Trafford	13	12
Hunslet	14	12
Keighley	13	12
Whitehaven	13	12

ROUND-UP

The fixture list was packed with games taking advantage of the Christmas festivities, with most being played on Boxing day.

At the week-end; *Bradford Northern* became the first team to reach a major final in the year when they booked their slot in the Regal Trophy final at the expense of *Rochdale*. Northern's defence was again on form and Rochdale rarely came close to scoring in a fairly dour match.

David Mycoe helped *Sheffield Eagles* finally land a win over *St Helens* despite the visitors leading at half-time through tries by Les Quirk and Sean Devine. *Wigan* were lucky to find a defence as weak as *Leed's*, otherwise they would have struggled to get their two points in a game where both teams looked indecisive.

Huddersfield recorded their highest score of the season against *Whitehaven* with the help of four tries from Ian Thomas and a Wally Gibson hat-trick. *Carlisle* rushed six tries in the second half to defeat *Batley*, Kevin Pace starting the charge with a try from 60 yards out. Gary Barnett nearly earned *Bramley* a draw at *Doncaster* with an injury-time try, but Steve Carroll failed to convert. *Keighley* were reduced to 12 men when Ray Priestley was sent off for stamping, but they still eased a win against *Chorley*.

Festive Fixtures

On Boxing day the weather was fairly foul with even the spectators deserving medals for venturing out into the wind and the rain. The victors were generally the team who made the least handling errors; *Castleford* dropped Leigh Crooks and Keith England for disciplinary reasons and their absence proved disastrous as they caved in to *Hull*. Paul Harkin produced some excellent play against his old club as *Leeds* scored 20 points without reply in the first 30 minutes to sink *Bradford*.

Warrington sank deeper into trouble losing to *Widnes* in a bad tempered warm-up for the second Regal Trophy semi-final. The result was in doubt until the end at Post Office Road with Deryck Fox edging the game for *Featherstone* against *Wakefield* with some excellent tactical kicking. *Oldham* played the first half against the wind and then capitalised on tiredness in the second half with three tries to beat *Rochdale*. *Wigan* came from behind twice, to beat *St Helens* and to jump into third place in the division.

Forward Mark Faumina tackled out of his skin and produced some powerful runs to enable *Ryedale-York* to register a win over *Doncaster* as revenge for their Regal Trophy defeat. Chris Wilkinson landed the only goal of the game as *Dewsbury* won a lottery against *Batley*. *Barrow* scored a surprise victory over *Carlisle* highlighted by a length-of-the-field try by full-back Pat Trainor. Greg Austin got his 23rd try of the season to help *Halifax* beat *Keighley*.

Freak Accident

Jonathan Davies was put out of action for a month following a freak training accident. Davies slipped on a wet pitch while practising his goal-kicking causing the rupture of thigh muscles.

League Settle Disputes

Bramley's boxing day game against Hunslet was called off only 50 minutes before the kick-off time because of a water logged pitch. Whilst Bramley were prepared to play, Hunslet thought that the pitch was unfit. The clubs also disagreed about the replay date. Bramley proposed that the game should go ahead on 30th when both teams had an open date, but Hunslet rejected this because the clubs Christmas party was being held on the 29th. The Rugby League ruled that the game should be played on the Sunday (30th) with a kick-off at 2:15pm.

Forwards Fined

Castleford imposed fines on their wayward forwards Lee Crooks and Keith England, who had been dropped for their visit to Hull as a result of the two missing training on the 21st. The hefty fines were imposed by coach Darryl Van De Velde who called the incident closed after both forwards trained on Christmas Eve and Christmas Day.

Calculated Provocation

Bradford player-coach David Hobbs complained that Leeds' players deliberately provoked Bradford players, because they knew the Bradford players would not want to risk a suspension for the Regal Trophy final if they retaliated. Although Hobbs accepted that this was 'standard practice' he was disappointed at the lack of protection given by referee Mr Kershaw.

December 29th - January 4th (1991)

RESULTS

REGALTROPHY-Semifinal

Widnes	4	Warrington	8

DIVISION 1

Castleford	9	Bradford	0 bh
Hull KR	16	Sheffield	16
Hull KR	20	Hull	8 bh
Leeds	28	Oldham	12 bh
Wakefield	8	Featherstone	16
Widnes	14	St Helens	8 bh
Wigan	6	Warrington	14 bh

	P	Pts
Widnes	12	20
Hull	13	20
Leeds	13	16
Hull KR	14	16
Wigan	12	15
Bradford	14	14
Castleford	13	14
Featherstone	13	13
Wakefield	11	12
St Helens	12	10
Warrington	14	10
Oldham	14	10
Sheffield	13	8
Rochdale	12	2

DIVISION 2

Batley	12	Dewsbury	6 bh
Bramley	14	Hunslet	26
Carlisle	10	Whitehaven	14
Chorley	9	Trafford	8 bh
Halifax	40	Doncaster	16 bh
Huddersfield	8	Keighley	10 bh
Hunslet	30	Bramley	18 bh
Runcorn	11	Leigh	32 bh
Ryedale-York	34	Barrow	0
Salford	13	Swinton	0 bh
Workington	29	Whitehaven	6

	P	Pts
Salford	13	26
Ryedale-York	16	25
Halifax	15	24
Swinton	13	22
Carlisle	15	21
Leigh	13	20
Huddersfield	14	17
Workington	14	17
Hunslet	16	16
Fulham	13	16
Keighley	14	14
Doncaster	15	14
Whitehaven	15	14
Trafford	14	12

ROUNDUP

Warrington had a splendid week with victories over both *Widnes* and *Wigan*. First they outplayed Widnes in the second semi-final of the Regal Trophy; Chris Rudd scoring all the points with a try and two penalties, after Widnes had taken the lead with a try against the run of play despite suspicions of a forward pass. Then they recorded their win over Wigan in the league with winger Mark Foster scoring an 80 yard interception try in his first appearance of the season, and Basil Richards scoring a try in his first minute on the pitch.

Castleford got the better of a mistake ridden game containing 32 scrums in awful conditions to overcome *Bradford*. *Leeds* scored all four of their tries in the second half to come back from 8-12 down against *Oldham*. *Widnes* overcame their Regal Trophy exit to register a win over neighbours *St Helens*. *Hull* surrendered their top spot to Widnes when they lost a hard game to their neighbours *Hull KR*.

Featherstone completed a holiday double over *Wakefield* with two tries from Ikram Butt and one by Ian Smales. *Sheffield* picked up another valuable point with their second draw of the season, this time at home to *Hull KR*.

Ryedale-York briefly moved to the top of the second division with a comprehensive win over *Barrow*, thanks in part to top points scorer Graham Sullivan who bagged two tries and five goals. However, *Salford* reclaimed the top spot with a 13-0 win over close rivals *Swinton* in their 13th win of the season. *Halifax* kept their promotion hopes alive with a victory over *Doncaster*, but they looked far from first division material in the first half when the visitors took the lead twice.

Oldham Close-down

Oldham were ordered to close their main stand until essential safety work was completed on the roof. Extra workmen were called in to get the roof ready for their next game against Featherstone on 6th January.

Gallagher Opts for Britain

Ex-New Zealand All Black, John Gallagher, who had been involved in a tug-of-war between New Zealand and Great Britain to pledge his Rugby League loyalty to them, decided in favour of the Lions.

London born Gallagher said that the decision had been made easier for him because he had started studies for a sports degree at Carnegie College in Leeds. In explanation, he said that if he had decided in favour of New Zealand then he would have been away from his studies for too long. The Leeds full-back added that it would be a great honour to be considered for the Great Britain team.

Leigh Sued

Hooker Mick Dean was planning to sue the Second Division club for non payment of contract money owing to him. This added more financial worries to Leigh who had debts of £900,000 and who had recently had three players walk out.

Reserve Brawl

Featherstone and Oldham were reported to the Rugby League after a brawl during the Friday night Slalom Lager Alliance reserve team match between the clubs. Three players were sent off following the exchange of blows just before half time - Oldham's scrum-half Neil Flanagan, and second row forward Keith Newton plus an unnamed trialist for Featherstone

The Action Sport

The RL produced a promotional video to help encourage the development of the game entitled "An Introduction to Rugby League - The Action Sport". The video was distributed nationally and became available free of charge to local authorities and interested sports bodies.

More Trouble at Hull KR

Hull Kingston Rovers put their full-back David Lightfoot onto the transfer list at £40,000 after he missed Christmas training.

January 5th - January 11th

RESULTS

DIVISION 1

Bradford	23	Rochdale	16
Castleford	20	Widnes	10
Hull	34	Leeds	14
Oldham	18	Featherstone	20
Rochdale	12	Featherstone	26 mw
St Helens	36	Wakefield	14
Sheffield	4	Wigan	46
Warrington	30	Hull KR	12

DIVISION 2

Barrow	10	Keighley	14
Chorley	19	Huddersfield	6
Dewsbury	2	Salford	50
Doncaster	58	Bramley	2
Fulham	13	Trafford	6
Hunslet	17	Whitehaven	8
Leigh	4	Salford	20 mw
Nottingham	15	Batley	16
Runcorn	0	Halifax	62
Swinton	12	Ryedale-York	6
Swinton	12	Trafford	10 mw
Workington	10	Leigh	3

	P	Pts
Hull	14	22
Widnes	13	20
Wigan	13	17
Featherstone	15	17
Leeds	14	16
Bradford	15	16
Castleford	14	16
Hull KR	15	16
St Helens	13	12
Warrington	15	12
Wakefield	12	12
Oldham	15	10
Sheffield	14	8
Rochdale	14	2

	P	Pts
Salford	14	28
Halifax	16	26
Ryedale-York	17	25
Swinton	14	24
Carlisle	15	21
Leigh	14	20
Workington	15	19
Hunslet	17	18
Fulham	14	18
Huddersfield	15	17
Doncaster	16	16
Keighley	15	16
Whitehaven	16	14
Trafford	15	12

ROUNDUP

Castleford created the main surprise of the day with a victory over *Widnes*. Leading 14-0 just five minutes after half-time, Castleford had to keep cool during a spirited Chemics fightback but an interception by Graham Steadman in the Widnes 25 yard area produced a try for Dean Sampson to seal the win. *Hull* gave Brian Smith a farewell present with a comprehensive victory over *Leeds*. It was another Australian, Greg Mackey who lead the home side to victory with involvement in four of Hull's six tries.

      Bradford looked to be doing just enough to beat *Rochdale* without picking up any injuries for their Regal trophy final. *Warrington*, the other finalists, looked more impressive with a resounding six-try win over *Hull KR*. *Wigan* dished out *Sheffield's* heaviest defeat of the season with six tries, Ellery Hanley got two taking his career total to 301. *Wakefield* lost to *St Helens* after losing Chris Perry to the sin bin for obstruction on Phil Veivers. Owen Simpson clinched victory for *Featherstone* in a tight game against *Oldham*, he also got a try in their midweek victory over *Rochdale*. Oldham claimed that Rovers' centre Terry Manning had been tackled and then got back on to his feet to continue the move which led to the winning try.

      Swinton got the best of *Ryedale-York* in their top four clash, with the visitors not being able to match the power of the home forwards. *Salford* kept up their 100% record with a nine try win at *Dewsbury*. In their second game of the week, *Salford* had an easy win at *Leigh*, and *Swinton* had a close call at home to *Trafford*. *Doncaster* produced a big score against *Bramley* to record a new record club victory. *Halifax* also went on a try scoring spree against bottom of the table *Runcorn* with 12 tries and seven goals.

Teams of the Month

Warrington and Keighley gained the Stones Bitter Teams of the Month Awards for December. Both teams had shown improved form, Warrington reached the Regal Trophy final and beat Widnes in the league whilst Keighley got back onto the winning track after gaining only one point from their previous seven games.

Transfer Disagreement

Leigh and St Helens found that they could not agree terms over the transfer of full-back Paul Topping from Leigh to Saints. Leigh wanted £40,000 plus Saints centre Tony Kay and winger David Tanner or forward Andy Bateman. St Helens said that they would not go ahead with the signing unless Leigh dropped their demands.

Recognition

Mark Brook-Cowden won his battle to be recognised as a British player, even though he played for the New Zealand All-Blacks. He holds a British passport and played his first Rugby League in Britain, turning professional for Leeds in 1986, although he was released by Salford during the summer of 1990.

Record Entry

The BNFL National Cup attracted a record entry of 225 amateur teams. The cup final was scheduled for May 19th at Knowsley Road, the home of St Helens RLFC.

Then There Would be Three

The Rugby League announced that it was aiming to have three divisions by the 1992/93 season. Spokesman David Howes confirmed the plans and said that all clubs needed to know what to aim at in the season 1991/92 before the three division format came into being.

36th Club

Scarborough Football Club got the go-ahead to start the country's 36th professional Rugby League club. Their application was narrowly approved, needing two thirds approval, only 30 of the existing 35 clubs turned up at the meeting with 20 voting in favour of Scarborough and 10 against.

January 12th - January 18th

RESULTS

REGAL TROPHY - Final

Warrington 12   Bradford 2

DIVISION 1

Featherstone 28	St Helens 36
Hull KR 42	Oldham 14
Leeds 38	Sheffield 16
Wakefield 12	Warrington 12 mw

DIVISION 2

Bramley 12   Batley 28

	P	Pts
Hull	14	22
Widnes	13	20
Leeds	15	18
Hull KR	16	18
Wigan	13	17
Featherstone	16	17
Bradford	15	16
Castleford	14	16
St Helens	14	14
Warrington	16	13
Wakefield	13	13
Oldham	16	10
Sheffield	15	8
Rochdale	14	2

	P	Pts
Salford	15	30
Halifax	16	26
Swinton	15	26
Ryedale-York	17	25
Carlisle	15	21
Leigh	15	20
Workington	15	19
Hunslet	17	18
Fulham	14	18
Huddersfield	15	17
Doncaster	16	16
Keighley	15	16
Whitehaven	16	14
Trafford	16	12

ROUNDUP

Warrington became the first major trophy winners of the season when they beat *Bradford* in a very dour final at Headingley. Both sides opted to play a forward's game and excitement was hard to come by as the two heavyweight packs cancelled one another out. Warrington's Mark Thomas got the only try on the full time hooter, the rest of the points being kicked.

The Sunday programme was severely curtailed as waterlogged pitches froze solid - only three matches in Division One and one in Division Two survived.

Featherstone threw away a 28-14 half time lead to go down to a *St Helens* side who had asked the referee to abandon the game at the break because of injuries on the hard ground.

Leeds overpowered *Sheffield* in the first half and then lost their way a little when Paul Harkin was replaced. *Hull KR* registered a big win against *Oldham* with veteran centre John Lydiat scoring two tries.

Bramley's home game against *Batley* was the only surviving game in Division Two, but the home side probably wished it wasn't when they lost two players with injury and had one dismissed. All attempts to replay games during the week failed due to the same icy conditions with the exception of *Wakefield* v *Warrington* who played out a draw.

Barrow Sacked

Oldham sacked their coach Tony Barrow after sinking into the relegation zone with just one win from their last nine games. Barrow had been in charge at The Roughyeds since November 1988 and still had a season and a half to run on his contract. John Fieldhouse, the Oldham pack leader, was put in temporary charge.

Later in the week, Ian Taylor, the second team coach resigned in protest at the sacking of Barrow. Gary Hyde, the team's veteran centre, was asked to take over his position. Ex-Great Britain coach Maurice Bamford also said that he would be helping the club in an advisory role.

Simpson Call up

In the week in which allied forces in the Gulf started attacking Iraq, Featherstone Rovers' winger Owen Simpson faced call-up only two months after joining the club. Simpson's name was on the Army reserve list after leaving the Duke of Wellington Regiment to join Keighley Rugby League club.

Keighley had spotted Simpson, aged 23, playing Rugby Union for the Army and had paid £600 to secure his release. Featherstone later paid £50,000 for his transfer in November 1990.

More Bad Luck

St Helen's forward Paul Forber looked set to return to training following another injury to his neck. After having four scans in less than five months he was told that another injury would almost certainly mean surgery would be required. However, the prospect of a neck injury from playing rugby receded when the unlucky player broke a leg while doing his daytime job.

Stanton Quandary

Frank Stanton, heavily tipped to take over from Roger Millward as coach of Hull KR at the end of the season, prepared to leave for Australia. Stanton said that he had still not made up his mind whether to take up the job, despite having long wanted to coach an English club. He explained that he still had to consult his employers and his wife's business partner in addition to considering his children's education.

Young Blood

BARLA's Young Lions clocked up a 24-6 win over France in Bordeaux. The Under-19's led with solid defence work which helped them in this record win.

January 19th - January 25th

RESULTS

DIVISION 1

Castleford 30	Hull KR 2
Castleford 42	Rochdale 0 mw
Hull 34	Bradford 6
Oldham 26	Wakefield 22
Sheffield 30	Rochdale 16
St Helens 22	Leeds 16
Warrington 16	Featherstone 10
Widnes 14	Wigan 22

	P	Pts
Hull	15	24
Widnes	14	20
Castleford	16	20
Wigan	14	19
Leeds	16	18
Hull KR	17	18
Featherstone	17	17
St Helens	15	16
Bradford	16	16
Warrington	17	15
Wakefield	14	13
Oldham	17	12
Sheffield	16	10
Rochdale	16	2

DIVISION 2

Batley 0	Halifax 12
Doncaster 32	Dewsbury 14
Fulham 20	Leigh 23
Huddersfield 12	Swinton 21
Hunslet 14	Chorley 14
Keighley 4	Carlisle 30
Nottingham 14	Whitehaven 28
Runcorn 6	Trafford 10
Salford 22	Ryedale-York 12
Salford 50	Runcorn 6
Whitehaven 20	Nottingham 10 mw
Workington 52	Bramley 9

	P	Pts
Salford	17	34
Halifax	17	28
Swinton	16	28
Ryedale-York	18	25
Carlisle	16	23
Leigh	16	22
Workington	16	21
Hunslet	18	19
Doncaster	17	18
Fulham	15	18
Whitehaven	18	18
Huddersfield	16	17
Keighley	16	16
Trafford	17	14

ROUNDUP

Ellery Hanley appeared to be a class apart from the rest as he scored a hat-trick for *Wigan* to win at *Widnes* despite having Andy Gregory sent off for biting. *Hull KR* lost four players with injury, ending up with only 11 men on the pitch as they went down at *Castleford*. *Hull* finished their game against *Bradford* with only 12 players but this was because prop Karl Harrison was sent off for a high tackle, even so they ran out easy winners.

 Wakefield suffered from the pent up anguish in the *Oldham* camp, the home side coming back from 0-10 down with three tries in five minutes. Gary Hetherington rallied his players with tough talking, to sting the *Eagles* into a win over *Rochdale*.

 Leeds full-back John Gallagher was stretchered off the pitch after a hard tackle and *St Helens* took advantage to swing the game their way. Form team *Warrington* defeated *Featherstone* with their full-back David Lyon scoring a try and four goals.

Ryedale-York gave away four penalties in front of their posts as they lost their top of the table game against *Salford*. Centre Greg Austin got *Halifax's* second try to relieve their battered defence from some strain against *Batley*. Prop Steve Brierly scored the first try for *Carlisle* in their victory at *Keighley*.

Coach Quits

Alan Agar quit as coach of Rochdale Hornets after achieving only one win in fifteen following promotion to the first division. Agar had not only guided The Hornets to promotion but also to the semi-finals of the Regal Trophy during his 18 months in charge after taking over from Jim Crellin.

Drugs Probe

The RFL said that a player would be appearing before the disciplinary committee to explain traces of the drug 'amphetamine' in a sample taken from a player after the boxing day game between Leeds and Bradford.

The League said that a few players had failed the test since the introduction of random testing but all had produced satisfactory explanations and been found 'not guilty'. This was the first case to become known to the public.

Prop Simon Tuffs of Bradford Northern was later discovered to be the player concerned. In defence, he claimed that he must have had one of his drinks 'spiked' at a Christmas Eve party 48 hours before the game.

The disciplinary committee heard the evidence and decided to seek further advice and to delay judgement until a later date.

To Bite or not to Bite

Andy Gregory was sent off by referee Colin Morris during Wigan's game at Widnes for allegedly biting. However, Kurt Sorenson, the supposed victim of the biting, said that he was not aware of anyone biting him and he could not find any bite marks on him the next morning.

Wigan coach John Monie apologised during the next week to the league disciplinary committee, and to Mr Morris, for his criticism of the sending-off decision.

Harrison Ban

Karl Harrison received a four match ban for his sending of against Bradford. The ban was imposed despite defence from Bradford's Craig Richards, the player who was high tackled by Harrison.

Harrison appealed unsuccessfully which meant that he would not be eligible for the test squad to play France, nor for the opening rounds of the Challenge Cup. Ian Lucas of Wigan replaced him in the test squad

Maurice Move

Ex-Great Britain coach Maurice Bamford resigned from his advisory role to Oldham, only a week after accepting the position, following his appointment as Bramley's general manager.

January 26th - February 1st

RESULTS

DIVISION 1

Featherstone 28	Oldham 20
Hull KR 26	St Helens 26
Leeds 20	Warrington 20
Rochdale 6	Widnes 60
Wakefield 8	Castleford 12

DIVISION 2

Bramley 16	Barrow 14
Doncaster 12	Salford 14 mw
Hunslet 6	Batley 0
Leigh 18	Workington 12 mw
Ryedale-York 22	Fulham 4
Swinton 16	Nottingham 4
Whitehaven 22	Runcorn 14

	P	Pts
Hull	15	24
Widnes	15	22
Castleford	17	22
Wigan	14	19
Leeds	17	19
Featherstone	18	19
Hull KR	18	19
St Helens	16	17
Warrington	18	16
Bradford	16	16
Wakefield	15	13
Oldham	18	12
Sheffield	16	10
Rochdale	17	2

	P	Pts
Salford	18	36
Swinton	17	30
Halifax	17	28
Ryedale-York	19	27
Leigh	17	24
Carlisle	16	23
Workington	17	21
Hunslet	19	21
Whitehaven	19	20
Doncaster	18	18
Fulham	16	18
Huddersfield	16	17
Keighley	16	16
Trafford	17	14

ROUNDUP

Great Britain travelled to **France** for an under-21 international at Limoux and a World Cup qualifying Test at Perpignon. The British teams ran in eight tries in both games to register easy wins. Wigan's Phil Clarke took the man-of-the-match award for the under-21's whilst Leeds' Garry Schofield was the inspiration of the grown-ups.

The Challenge Cup got under-way; League leaders *Hull* suffered the biggest shock when they went out to *Sheffield*. Each of the amateur clubs made their opponents fight, most notably *Leigh East* who came to within 8-12 of *Bradford* at Second Division Leigh's ground.

In the leagues; Terry Manning scored two tries for *Featherstone* to sink *Oldham's* fightback. *Castleford* defeated *Wakefield* when Lee Crooks scored against the run of play. Les Quirk scored with three minutes to go, giving *St Helens* a 26-20 lead only to see David Watson grab the points back for *Hull KR* in an exciting draw. Another heavily anticipated draw at Headingley saw *Warrington* virtually kill off *Leeds'* championship hopes. Ben Lia scored two tries in his debut for *Widnes* during their big win at *Rochdale*.

Junior Discipline

A two man disciplinary committee decided that sending-offs were sufficient for Darren Moxon of Great Britain and Christopher Grandjean of France, following their dismissal for brawling in the under-21 International.

Tuuta Stays

New Zealand international loose-forward Brendon Tuuta signed a new two year contract with Featherstone Rovers. The 25 year old arrived at Post Office Road in August 1990 on a short term contract which was due to finish after Featherstone's game against Oldham on 3rd February. However, Rovers contacted his Australian club Western Suburbs and arranged to buy out his contract.

Honorary Positions

The French Rugby League Federation made Bob Ashby and David Oxley (Chairman and Chief Executive of the British RFL) honorary life members of their federation in recognition of all the help they had given.

Free Play

In a bid to get Papua New Guinea to play a game at Mount Pleasant, the Batley players offered to turn out and play for nothing.

Tackle Review

Leeds requested the Controller of Referees, Fred Lindop, to look at the tackle made by St Helens on their full-back John Gallagher. They claimed that the tackle which had damaged Gallagher's neck was an illegal 'spear' tackle in which he was deliberately driven head-first into the ground.

Leeds' club doctor and physiotherapist both gave Gallagher the go-ahead to play later in the week after studying x-rays.

New Kit

A debate opened as to whether the British Coal sponsored International jersey should be changed in order to cash in on the lucrative market of replica kits. The existing kit was proving to be very popular with the public, but it was said it could do with a facelift.

February 2nd - February 8th

RESULTS

DIVISION 1

Castleford 16	Leeds 14		
Hull 28	Rochdale 8		
Oldham 16	St Helens 20		
Sheffield 24	Featherstone 27		
Warrington 12	Bradford 13		
Wigan 34	Hull KR 4 mw		
Widnes 34	Wakefield 6		

	P	Pts
Hull	16	26
Widnes	16	24
Castleford	18	24
Wigan	15	21
Featherstone	19	21
Leeds	18	19
St Helens	17	19
Hull KR	19	19
Bradford	17	18
Warrington	19	16
Wakefield	16	13
Oldham	19	12
Sheffield	17	10
Rochdale	18	2

DIVISION 2

Batley 40	Bramley 16		
Chorley 12	Leigh 30		
Fulham 26	Swinton 10		
Nottingham 2	Keighley 24		
Runcorn 12	Carlisle 12		
Trafford 25	Doncaster 29		
Workington 28	Huddersfield 17		

	P	Pts
Salford	18	36
Swinton	18	30
Halifax	17	28
Ryedale-York	19	27
Leigh	18	26
Carlisle	17	24
Workington	18	23
Hunslet	19	21
Doncaster	19	20
Fulham	17	20
Whitehaven	19	20
Keighley	17	18
Huddersfield	17	17
Trafford	18	14

ROUNDUP

Wigan took only 90 seconds to open the scoring in their win against *Hull KR* through Joe Lydon and then continued the surge to take a 16-0 lead in the first 15 minutes.

Bradford gained revenge over *Warrington* for their loss in the Regal Trophy Final in a totally different game with plenty of open play and excitement.

Graham Steadman scored a penalty with five minutes left to sink *Leeds* after the visitors had gained a 0-8 lead in the 24th minute in the match at *Castleford*.

Martin Offiah scored a hat-trick in *Widnes'* convincing win over *Wakefield*.

Featherstone scored five tries to win a high-scoring, close game at *Sheffield*.

The big news in the second division came at *Runcorn* versus *Carlisle*, when a last minute penalty by Norman Barrow gained the home side their first league point since January 22nd 1989 and after 61 straight league defeats.

There was another surprise in London where *Fulham* gained two points at the cost of *Swinton*.

January Teams

Castleford were named as the First Division team of the month for January after a winning run of five games which took them from ninth in the league to third.

Ray Ashton's Workington side took the award in the Second Division after improved league form and a close match with Bradford Northern in the Regal Trophy.

Ellis Call-up

Welsh scrum-half Kevin Ellis was called in to the Great Britain squad for the return U-21 Test against France. As the only un-capped player. Ellis had made a big impact with Warrington since his signing from Bridgend in May 1990 but had only played in 18 first team outings for the Wire.

Paul Loughlin of St Helens was re-called into the squad along with Karl Harrison of Hull and David Hulme of Widnes. Carl Gibson (Leeds), Tony Sullivan (Hull KR), Mark Aston (Sheffield) and Paul Hulme (Widnes) were dropped.

Step 2 to 3

The Rugby League Council members gave their backing to the concept of three divisions as proposed by Sheffield's Gary Hetherington. The plan for a first division of 14 clubs, with eight in the second division and 14 in the third division, was then passed to a Special General Meeting to be held in Leeds on the 6th March.

Wally Lewis is Coming

The former Australian Test captain, Wally Lewis, made his debut with Australian club Gold Coast Giants but was hit on the head by a beer can thrown from the crowd. The wound reportedly needed five stitches and the police arrested the fan responsible.

Wigan Coaches

Current Wigan coach John Monie denied rumours that he was going to quit Central Park to return down-under as coach to Sydney club Parramatta.

Ex-coach Graham Lowe went into hospital to undergo surgery for the removal of a blood clot from his brain.

Not So Funny Bone

Paul Newlove at Featherstone broke his elbow in the Sunday fixture and looked to be out of the team for at least six weeks.

February 9th - February 15th

RESULTS

CHALLENGE CUP - 1st round

Castleford 4	Wigan 28 mw
Doncaster 4	Widnes 30
Keighley 36	Runcorn 4 mw
Leeds 40	Dewsbury 20
Salford 36	Batley 14 mw
Swinton 8	St Helens 18

DIVISION 2

Hunslet 56	Barrow 4

UNDER-21 INTERNATIONAL

Great Britain 6	France 16

ROUNDUP

Arctic weather and some of the heaviest snow for many years hampered the full programme with most matches being called-off.

Matches that went ahead at the week-end; *St Helens* lost Sean Devine after six minutes with a dislocated ankle and Jonathan Griffiths after nine minutes with knee trouble but still made it into the Challenge Cup second round, at the expense of Second Division high-fliers *Swinton.*

Leeds claimed their spot in the second round with a win at home to *Dewsbury* thanks to 28 points in the space of 18 minutes mid-way through the second half.

Widnes also entered the second round by beating *Doncaster* who had matched the Chemics blow-for-blow in the first half.

The only game to survive the weather in the second division saw *Hunslet* revelling in an 11 try party against *Barrow* but only 434 fans turned up to watch the game.

During the week; *Wigan* indicated the strength of their challenge for a fourth Wembley victory with a win over *Castleford* after rushing to a 22-0 lead at half-time, Frano Botica scoring two tries and three goals.

Keighley deflated *Runcorn's* and the press entourage's hopes of a win for the leagues' bottom club, helped by the fact that the visitors had to play with 12 men for most of the second half through injury. *Salford* beat *Batley* with help from six goals by Steve Kerry.

France turned their record under-21 defeat in Limoux into a surprise victory at Wigan against *Great Britain* U-21s. Despite taking the lead in the sixth minute, Britain looked short of ideas and imagination as Pascal Fages drew France level and winger Eric van Brussel added a further two tries.

Rough and Tumble

St Helen's scrum-half Sean Devine looked likley to miss the rest of the Rugby League season. He broke his ankle in Sunday's match.

Featherstone's Chris Bibb was also expected to be out of action for at least a month with a broken shoulder.

Inept

St Helens coach, Mike McLennan, described his side's performance against Swinton as inept, despite the Saints becoming the first side to qualify for the second round of the Challenge Cup. After further attacks on the side's performance he hinted that he may quit the club before his contract finished in May 1992.

Meanwhile Sean Devine was ruled out of the team for the rest of the season after breaking his ankle in three places.

Mann Victory

George Mann won his appeal to the New Zealand Rugby League for a long term contract to play in Great Britain after being offered a three year contract at St Helens.

Classy Dressing

Great Britain and France were told that they would be the first teams to use the new changing rooms at Headingley. The new rooms, part of a £2.5 million development, were described by players as the best in the Rugby League world.

Confidence

Widnes decided to go-ahead with their game against Leeds (on the 17th) despite having six of their players on duty for Great Britain in the Test or the under-21 International against France.

Youngsters Disappointment

The under-21 International against France, which had been awarded to Huddersfield for ground improvements, was switched to Wigan's Central Park because of the poor weather conditions. Huddersfield's ground was thought to be too exposed and prone to bad weather, whilst Central Park had under-pitch heating.

More than 1,000 schoolchildren had been given invitations to watch the match at Huddersfield.

Casey coach

Len Casey, ex-Great Britain, Hull, Hull KR, Bradford and Wakefield coach, was named as the coach for newcomers Scarborough with a three year contract at the club.

Sacked

Barrow sacked coach Steve Norton after a run of losses which left them fourth bottom of the second division.

February 16th - February 22nd

RESULTS

ROUNDUP

Great Britain scored a record-breaking win over *France* at Headingley. Martin Offiah scored five magnificent tries from the wing, Garry Schofield scored three to reach a total of 25 tries for his country and Paul Eastwood scored eight successive goals followed by five successive misses. Despite the score-line, Great Britain didn't have it all their own way, with France putting in a good first half to go in only 16-0 down. However in the second half the GB team turned on the screws and saw an eventual French collapse.

Workington pulled out the surprise that they had been threatening with a victory over *Hull KR* to enter the second round of the Challenge Cup. To make things worse it was one of Rovers' ex-players, Colin Armstrong, who scored the first try and inspired Workington to a second half come-back.

There were a couple of revenge games; *Sheffield* sent *Featherstone* out with a tough tackling performance and tries early in both halves. *Barrow*, who sacked their coach after their embarrassing league defeat at *Hunslet*, turned their game around to surprise the visitors.

Ryedale-York gave *Warrington* a fright before they lost to two second half tries by David Lyon and Duane Mann. It wasn't as close at Valley Parade, where *Bradford Northern* got inspiration from re-locating to Bradford City's soccer ground, in a nine try romp with 12 points in the first 11 minutes against *Leigh*. This was the best display by Northern for a few weeks and gave them a home fixture against Leeds in the Silk Cut Challenge Cup second round tie.

Trafford were still in contention at 12-7 down with four minutes to go against *Wakefield* before the home side stopped squandering their chances and sealed the game. The score suggested that *Halifax* walked into the second round against *Fulham*, however virtually nobody could walk let-alone run on a pitch that resembled a muddy swamp.

In the leagues; *Widnes'* confidence paid off by playing *Leeds* despite having had players on duty for their country when they devastated the home side with seven tries, Andy Currier scoring three tries and five goals for 22 points. Martin Offiah performed a 60 yard sprint to open the try scoring and make his 38th try of the season. He'd been in action for the GB team less than a day earlier.

Dewsbury coach Jack Addy, who left *Huddersfield* on poor terms, celebrated his team's first league win of 1991 at his old ground.

Apologies

Leeds' chief executive, Alf Davies, apologised to fans for having to pay good money to watch the Loiner's disgraceful performance against Widnes. He added that the absence of a few key players was not an excuse for the disgrace. Having the best facilities in the game was no substitute for performance, he commented.

London Amateurs

Hemel Hempstead, the London amateur champions for the past two seasons, applied to join the Alliance League as the initial step in a bid to join the full league in future years.

Gateshead Charity

Gateshead International Stadium, with a 11,500 capacity, was chosen as the venue for the 1991 Charity Shield to be held on 25th August. The choice was made as part of the League's policy of promoting the game in development areas.

No More Commitment

Barry Seaborne resigned as coach of Huddersfield after five consecutive losses due to the lack of commitment from his players. Chairman Jim Collins said that he was sorry to see Seaborne go after the tremendous amount of work he had put in.

Union Rules

Proposals were made to change scrummaging rules in Rugby Union and to reduce the value of a penalty goal to make the game more attractive to watch !

Bradford Bills

The accounts for the year to June 1990 were published this week and they showed a loss after tax of £57,478 against a profit for the previous year of £142,686. This was despite the team reaching two finals in that period. Chairman Chris Caisley commented that it was due to the soaring price of contract payments to players which increased by 86%.

February 23rd - March 1st

RESULTS

CHALLENGE CUP - 2nd round

Barrow	4	Widnes	28
Bradford	5	Leeds	0
Halifax	46	Whitehaven	12
Keighley	10	Warrington	42
Rochdale	4	Wigan	72
Sheffield	16	Salford	19
St Helens	16	Wakefield	2
Workington	15	Oldham	20

DIVISION 1

Bradford	6	Sheffield	10 mw
Hull KR	12	Castleford	16
Rochdale	10	Warrington	18 mw
Widnes	28	Hull	2 mw

DIVISION 2

Barrow	4	Hunslet	4 mw
Bramley	29	Nottingham	6
Carlisle	13	Batley	19
Chorley	2	Fulham	36
Halifax	32	Keighley	8 mw
Leigh	31	Hunslet	24
Leigh	12	Fulham	12 mw
Ryedale-York	12	Swinton	12
Salford	32	Dewsbury	6 mw
Trafford	23	Huddersfield	22
Whitehaven	2	Batley	18 mw

	P	Pts
Widnes	18	28
Hull	18	26
Castleford	19	26
Wigan	15	21
St Helens	18	21
Featherstone	19	21
Leeds	19	19
Hull KR	20	19
Warrington	20	18
Bradford	18	18
Wakefield	16	13
Oldham	19	12
Sheffield	18	12
Rochdale	19	2

	P	Pts
Salford	19	38
Swinton	20	33
Halifax	18	30
Ryedale-York	21	30
Leigh	20	29
Carlisle	19	24
Hunslet	22	24
Workington	18	23
Fulham	19	23
Doncaster	19	20
Keighley	19	20
Whitehaven	20	20
Batley	20	18
Huddersfield	20	17

ROUNDUP

Ellery Hanley scored six tries and Frano Botica scored 12 goals as *Wigan* demolished *Rochdale* to reach the quarter finals of the Challenge Cup. The second highest victory fell to *Halifax* as they fought back against two tries from visiting *Whitehaven* in the first 12 minutes. *Keighley* also crossed the try line first in going down to *Warrington* but Hayden Kelly was judged to have been held on his back.

Oldham had to fight off a determined *Workington* looking for their second First Division scalp. *Sheffield* put up only mild resistance to a determined onslaught by *Salford* and duly paid for it with Andy Burgess scoring the visitors best try from 45 yards out. Martin Offiah took his seasons aggregate to 40 tries when he scored two in *Widnes'* victory over *Barrow*. *Bradford* scored all their points in the first 25 minutes and then hung on to nil *Leeds* for their second week. *St Helens* survived a mid game surge from *Wakefield* with help from four goals by Paul Loughlin.

In the leagues; *Castleford* came back from 12-0 down after 50 minutes to score three tries in the next 10 minutes for victory over *Hull KR*. *Ryedale-York* also came back to tie their top three game in the Second Division against *Swinton*.

Tuffs Ban

Bradford Northern prop Simon Tuffs became the first player in British Rugby League history to be banned for failing a drugs test. The 23 year old was banned for two years after the RL rejected his claims about a spiked drink because of a lack of evidence.

Bradford Northern said that they would not take any action against Tuffs until the end of his 14 day appeal period in case of prejudice, although they viewed the matter very seriously.

Wigan scrum-half Andy Gregory made a call for the introduction of drug testing at all games in light of the incident.

More Red Ink

Oldham sank to £663,000 in the red after reporting a loss of £156,000 in the 89/90 season during which they gained promotion.

McClennan to Stay

Mike McClennan said that he would be staying with St Helens despite his threats to quit following the Saints narrow Challenge Cup victory over Swinton.

Rescue Bid Shelved

A consortium of four business men headed by a nightclub owner shelved their reported £40,000 rescue bid for Whitehaven.

Shaun Saved

Shaun Edwards' continuing run of 17 Challenge Cup victories (in association with Wigan of course) was saved when he was given only a one match suspension for punching in Wigan's game with Rochdale, which meant that he could play in Wigan's quarter-final against Bradford on 10th March.

Scarborough Name

League newcomers Scarborough, yet to tighten a boot lace, revealed that their name would be Scarborough Pirates when they started playing.

Take a Rest

Oldham and Great Britain under-21 player Tommy Martyn was advised not to play for at least a month following a series of blows to the head during the start to his first season at Oldham.

March 2nd - March 8th

RESULTS

DIVISION 1

Bradford	10	Oldham	37
Hull	40	Featherstone	22
Leeds	24	Hull KR	18
Rochdale	12	Castleford	76
Wakefield	12	Sheffield	4 mw
Warrington	34	St Helens	20
Wigan	16	Wakefield	8
Widnes	14	Sheffield	23

	P	Pts
Widnes	19	28
Hull	19	28
Castleford	20	28
Wigan	16	23
Leeds	20	21
St Helens	19	21
Featherstone	20	21
Warrington	21	20
Hull KR	21	19
Bradford	19	18
Wakefield	18	15
Oldham	20	14
Sheffield	20	14
Rochdale	20	2

DIVISION 2

Batley	4	Fulham	20
Chorley	22	Bramley	6
Doncaster	36	Whitehaven	0
Halifax	56	Whitehaven	6 mw
Huddersfield	18	Barrow	10
Keighley	10	Workington	15
Keighley	21	Salford	22
Runcorn	9	Dewsbury	2
Ryedale-York	18	Carlisle	12
Swinton	7	Leigh	6
Trafford	8	Halifax	39
Workington	38	Nottingham	4

	P	Pts
Salford	20	40
Swinton	21	35
Halifax	20	34
Ryedale-York	22	32
Leigh	21	29
Workington	20	27
Fulham	20	25
Hunslet	22	24
Carlisle	20	24
Doncaster	20	22
Keighley	21	20
Whitehaven	22	20
Huddersfield	21	19
Batley	21	18

ROUNDUP

It was the week of the lower clubs with *Runcorn* finally winning a game, their first in 78 games since 30th October 1988, *Dewsbury* will be remembered as the unfortunate team to break the run. At the lower end of the first division, *Sheffield* surprised top-of-the-table *Widnes* with a display of open football to lead 15-4 at half time and then to hold off a Widnes rally to 15-14. *Oldham* also threw the ball about to find gaps in an appalling *Bradford* defence with their scrum-half scoring two tries and setting up others. Not so lucky were *Rochdale* who watched *Castleford* run in 14 tries, stand-off Graham Steadman scoring 32 of his team's points.

    Leeds ended their bad run with a home win over *Hull KR,* in which they saw their 24-8 lead cut to 24-18 and desperately tried to get a drop goal before the hooter saved them. *Wakefield* battled hard against *Wigan* but finally went down to a try from Ellery Hanley six minutes from time. *Featherstone* lost to *Hull* but were not disgraced in a 12 try thriller, the visitors scoring in the first three minutes of both halves. David Lyon kicked seven goals and scored a try to help *Warrington* beat *St Helens.*

Subritzky dropped a goal for *Swinton* to break the second half deadlock against *Leigh* after both teams had gone in with six points a piece. Dixon's drop goal wasn't quite enough to earn *Keighley* a draw against *Salford*. Nick Pinkney scored two tries to keep *Ryedale-York* in touch with the leaders against *Carlisle.*

Status Quo Rules

A meeting of the existing 35 professional clubs failed to reach a 60% majority needed to approve the move to a three division format. Gary Hetherington's plan for a 14-8-14 format was narrowly rejected, with 19 clubs voting for it, just less than the 21 required. A plan put forward by Whitehaven and Huddersfield for a 14-11-11 format was rejected by a larger majority.

Afterwards the RFL indicated that they still thought three divisions was the 'way to go' and announced plans to re-introduce the idea at a meeting in April with a few amendments.

Another Application

The RFL received another application to join the league, this time from the Stoke area. The Chairman of Trafford Borough was thought to be behind the bid to become the leagues' 37th club by the start of the 1991/92 season. The club hoped to be playing its games at a ground in the Hanley region.

Gridiron Rumpus

News broke that Ellery Hanley, the Great Britain captain, had signed to play for London Monarchs in the new World League of American Football with reports suggesting that Hanley would receive £50,000 per game. The Monarchs said that they hoped Hanley would make his debut for them during the Easter week-end.

Meanwhile, Wigan said that Hanley was under exclusive contract to them until the end of the Rugby League season. Agreement was later reached which allowed Hanley to play three or four games for the Monarchs if they gained prior permission from Wigan.

Early Return

With Rochdale Hornets already doomed to a return to the Second Division, they released scrum-half Stuart Galbraith a month early so that he could return back to New Zealand.

Espoirs Exit

BARLA's Young Lions put over five tries in their 20-2 win against the French Espoirs in the Youth International at Whitehaven.

Top Teams

The February Stones Bitter second division Team of the Month cheque for £350 went to Batley. Widnes took the First Division cheque, worth £500.

March 9th - March 15th

RESULTS

CHALLENGE CUP - quarter finals

Warrington 14	Widnes 26
Halifax 16	St Helens 24
Oldham 40	Salford 3
Wigan 32	Bradford 2

DIVISION 1

Bradford 12	Wakefield 10 mw
Featherstone 22	Warrington 8 mw
Rochdale 20	Leeds 34
Sheffield 20	Castleford 24
St Helens 33	Oldham 22 mw
Wakefield 26	Hull KR 6
Wigan 34	Hull 12 mw

	P	Pts
Castleford	21	30
Widnes	19	28
Hull	20	28
Wigan	17	25
Leeds	21	23
St Helens	20	23
Featherstone	21	23
Warrington	22	20
Bradford	20	20
Hull KR	22	19
Wakefield	20	17
Oldham	21	14
Sheffield	21	14
Rochdale	21	2

DIVISION 2

Bramley 14	Huddersfield 12
Carlisle 32	Keighley 18
Dewsbury 15	Hunslet 12
Fulham 6	Workington 7
Halifax 48	Barrow 10 mw
Leigh 16	Doncaster 20
Nottingham 20	Runcorn 14
Ryedale-York 24	Batley 12
Ryedale-York 24	Hunslet 10 mw
Salford 46	Chorley 2 mw
Trafford 20	Barrow 27
Whitehaven 21	Chorley 16

	P	Pts
Salford	21	42
Ryedale-York	24	36
Halifax	21	36
Swinton	21	35
Leigh	22	29
Workington	21	29
Carlisle	21	26
Fulham	21	25
Hunslet	24	24
Doncaster	21	24
Whitehaven	23	22
Keighley	22	20
Huddersfield	22	19
Batley	22	18

ROUNDUP

Cup favourites *Wigan* marched in to the semi-finals with a powerful display against a valiant *Bradford* side who just weren't good enough. Andy Gregory got the man-of-the-match for his inspiration. *Widnes* also reached the semi's thanks to two interception tries from Currier and Offiah to sink *Warrington's* hopes of reaching the final for a second consecutive year. *Oldham* proved too powerful for an injury hit *Salford*, running in seven tries to one. *St Helens* grabbed the last place in the draw with a neck-and-neck battle against *Halifax*, George Mann making the vital break for Paul Bishop to score.

Leeds went behind to *Rochdale* in the early stages but never really looked like losing thanks to the artistry of scrum-half Paul Harkin. *Castleford* went back to the top of the division with a narrow victory over *Sheffield*, Shaun Irwin's touchdown from a kick-through proving the decider. *Hull KR* fans staged a protest for the board to resign as their team lost to *Wakefield*, their fifth consecutive defeat.

During the week, Andy Gregory continued to shine as *Wigan* scored an important win over *Hull*. *St Helens* came back from 15-16 down at half-time to beat *Oldham*. *Bradford* held on despite a late *Wakefield* surge to win at Odsal. Mike Gregory returned to action in *Warrington's* defeat at *Featherstone*.

Doncaster recorded their first win at *Leigh* for 23 years to improve their top eight position hopes and to end the home side's chances of promotion. *Runcorn's* hopes of a second win were lost when *Nottingham's* Iain Bowie scored a try with two minutes to go, sending Runcorn back to the bottom of the division.

Eight Out Of Ten

Eight goals from ten attempts by Carlisle's full back Barry Vickers kept alive their hopes of finishing in the top three of the Second Division.
Meanwhile, Whitehaven were benefitting from three on-loan Carlisle players in their weekend win over Chorley.

Cheap Pirates

Scarborough Pirates announced 1,000 cut-price season tickets were to go on sale to help generate interest for the game in the area. The season tickets were priced at £25 for adults and £15 for pensioners and children. Grandstand tickets were priced at £45 for adults for access to matches at the McCain stadium.
The club's colours were also announced as royal purple and gold.

Hanley Starts Training

Ellery Hanley started training with the London Monarchs American Football team as a running-back and the coach said that he was picking up the basic aspects of the game very quickly.

Out of Retirement

Kevin Tamati, the Salford coach was forced out of retirement due to an injury crisis at the club. He made his return to the team in Salford's mid-week game against Chorley.

Points Given

Halifax were awarded two league points for their home game against Whitehaven. Although the match had been abandoned due to fog with ten minutes still to play, the league decided that the result should stand. Halifax were leading 56-6 at the time.

Dewsbury Move

Dewsbury announced that they were going to move in with their neighbours Batley for the 1991/92 season. Plans to sell their Crown Flatt ground to a housing company and to build a new £1 million stadium were being delayed by planning permission hold-ups.

March 16th - March 22nd

RESULTS

DIVISION 1

Hull	6	Wakefield	14
Hull KR	16	Leeds	28
Oldham	27	Sheffield	20
Rochdale	16	Wigan	44
St Helens	54	Featherstone	38
Widnes	25	Warrington	6 mw
Widnes	32	Bradford	12

DIVISION 2

Barrow	8	Fulham	20
Batley	22	Keighley	12
Bramley	10	Swinton	17
Chorley	13	Halifax	22
Dewsbury	16	Huddersfield	18
Doncaster	14	Carlisle	7
Doncaster	12	Halifax	6 mw
Nottingham	12	Trafford	48
Runcorn	16	Whitehaven	30
Salford	32	Batley	14 mw
Workington	7	Salford	0

	P	Pts
Widnes	21	32
Castleford	21	30
Hull	21	28
Wigan	18	27
Leeds	22	25
St Helens	21	25
Featherstone	22	23
Warrington	23	20
Bradford	21	20
Wakefield	21	19
Hull KR	23	19
Oldham	22	16
Sheffield	22	14
Rochdale	22	2

	P	Pts
Salford	23	44
Halifax	23	38
Swinton	22	37
Ryedale-York	24	36
Workington	22	31
Leigh	22	29
Doncaster	23	28
Fulham	22	27
Carlisle	22	26
Hunslet	24	24
Whitehaven	24	24
Huddersfield	23	21
Batley	24	20
Keighley	23	20

ROUNDUP

Prop Kelvin Skerrett was sent off for *Wigan* after a clash with hooker Martin Hall in their win over *Rochdale.*

Jonathan Davies scored four tries but only kicked two goals from seven attempts in *Widnes'* win over *Bradford.* He then continued to shine during *Widnes'* win over *Warrington* in mid-week.

John Gallagher scored two tries and made a try saving tackle in his return to the winning *Leeds* side at *Hull KR.* Garry Schofield was the inspiration behind the Loiner's five tries.

Sheffield Eagles lost out in their vital relegation battle with *Oldham*, giving away too many early points to trail 20-8 at half time, despite good play from Kiwi Des Maea

Featherstone also gave away too many points early on in their 16 try thriller at *St Helens,* they trailed by 38-4 before hitting back to 44-38 and then conceding two late tries.

Richard Slater scored the try for *Wakefield* to virtually end *Hull's* title hopes. It was Hull's first defeat of the season at the Boulevard.

Workington inflicted the first defeat of the season on *Salford* with a try by Kerr. *Halifax* struggled to overcome *Chorley* after going in 13-8 down at half-time and then lost to *Doncaster* in mid-week. *Swinton* also struggled against a *Bramley* side who held a narrow 10-9 lead at the break.

Testing Times

Referee John Holdsworth from Kippax was appointed referee for the forthcoming test series between Australia and New Zealand. The series, to be played in Australia, was scheduled to include a game in Melbourne which is a traditional Aussie-Rules Football stronghold. Other tests were lined up for the more traditional cities of Brisbane and Sydney. Mr Holdsworth had not refereed in Australia before his appointment.

Smith's Return Joy

Brian Smith, who left Hull in mid-season, had a good start to his first game in charge at Sydney St George with a 34-8 win over Parramatta.

Stoke Delay

Stoke's application to join the league as the 37th professional team was deferred for a year. The decision was made on the basis that the financial viability of the club was uncertain. When the decision was announced, the Stoke consortium said that they intended to re-submit their proposals in a different form before the end of the season.

Meanwhile Hemel Hempsted was given the go-ahead to become the first amateur side to compete in the Alliance League alongside the second teams of professional clubs.

Hanley Injury

Reports surfaced that Ellery Hanley had been injured during training with the London Monarchs American Football team. None of the reports were confirmed but Ellery started Wigan's Challenge Cup semi-final with heavy strapping on his knee.

Meeting Postponed

The RFL's second special meeting to re-introduce the idea of a new three division system was postponed for two weeks until 17th April to enable more teams to be represented.

Wakefield Breaks Record

Hull's unbeaten home record, which has stood since November 1989, was broken at the Boulevard by Wakefield Trinity.

March 23rd - March 29th

RESULTS

CHALLENGE CUP - Semi-final

Wigan 30	Oldham 16

DIVISION 1

Bradford 24	Castleford 14 mw
Castleford 28	St Helens 4
Featherstone 22	Widnes 27
Featherstone 16	Wigan 24 mw
Hull 28	Hull KR 16 mw
Hull KR 48	Rochdale 14
Leeds 7	Wakefield 0 mw
Rochdale 12	Oldham 30 mw
Sheffield 6	Hull 16
Wakefield 6	Bradford 16

DIVISION 2

Barrow 34	Nottingham 6 mw
Bramley 18	Salford 27
Chorley 20	Ryedale-York 24
Dewsbury 18	Runcorn 10
Fulham 28	Chorley 9 mw
Halifax 22	Workington 14
Huddersfield 22	Batley 0 mw
Hunslet 12	Swinton 16
Keighley 24	Barrow 20
Leigh 28	Batley 6
Nottingham 8	Doncaster 52
Ryedale-York 15	Doncaster 7 mw
Salford 18	Leigh 11 mw
Trafford 14	Carlisle 52
Trafford 10	Swinton 16 mw
Whitehaven 16	Fulham 20
Workington 12	Whitehaven 17 mw

	P	Pts		P	Pts
Widnes	22	34	Salford	25	48
Hull	23	32	Swinton	24	41
Castleford	23	32	Ryedale-York	26	40
Wigan	19	29	Halifax	24	40
Leeds	23	27	Leigh	24	31
St Helens	22	25	Workington	24	31
Bradford	23	24	Fulham	24	31
Featherstone	24	23	Doncaster	25	30
Hull KR	25	21	Carlisle	23	28
Warrington	24	20	Whitehaven	26	26
Wakefield	23	19	Hunslet	25	24
Oldham	23	18	Huddersfield	24	23
Sheffield	23	14	Keighley	24	22
Rochdale	24	2	Batley	26	20

ROUNDUP

Wigan looked to be running away with the first Challenge Cup semi-final against *Oldham* when they were 24-0 in the lead. However, John Fieldhouse asked his side to play for 'pride' and they outscored Wigan by three tries to one in the last half-hour.

   Widnes stayed at the top of the First Division, but only after a scare against *Featherstone*. The home side staged one of their strong come-backs after being down 2-16 at half time, but couldn't overcome Koloto's winning try for Widnes. *Castleford* gained revenge against *St Helens* for the Saints 'headed' tries earlier in the season. Graham Steadman kicked the ball straight forward from the play-the-ball over the Saints line and then dived on it to score.

   Sheffield fought hard against *Hull* and held them 6-6 at one stage but eventually folded in the second half. *Hull KR* proved too strong for *Rochdale* with Mike Fletcher getting six goals. *Bradford* scored two early tries against the run of play to lead *Wakefield* 6-10 but their big pack came good in the second half and Northern finished the stronger.

72

Second Division Rush

Dewsbury gave themselves an early 10 point lead over *Runcorn* to avoid another embarrassing defeat. *Swinton* had a tough game at *Hunslet* with Frodsham scoring two tries. *Ryedale-York* put two tries past *Chorley* at the start of the second half only to watch the home side come back, however they held out with a Williams try. Gibson scored two tries as *Salford* beat *Bramley* and clinched promotion to the first division.

The Easter games got under way on Good Friday; in a local derby *Hull* kept alive their championship hopes with a win over *Hull KR*. *Wigan* were troubled by *Featherstone Rovers* with Brendon Tuuta scoring one try and having a hand in the other two. Ellery Hanley limped off with an injured knee, but this did not stop a Wigan victory. Paul Medley's hat-trick of tries took *Bradford* to a storming win over *Castleford*. *Leeds* beat off sustained pressure from *Wakefield* to ensure a small victory. *Oldham* showed that they still had hopes of staying in the First Division with a win over *Rochdale* despite being involved in a 20 player brawl.

Salford's Steve Kerry kicked his 150th goal of the season in his team's win over *Leigh*. Tawera Nikau's pending departure from *Ryedale-York* resulted in a sterling performance from the New Zealander, ensuring a victory for his side against *Doncaster*.

Salford Rights

Salford announced plans to double their number of shares following their promotion to the first division. The move to raise extra capital came after they announced losses of £141,000 for the 89/90 season.

In, Out, Shake it all About

Mike McLennan confirmed that he would be leaving St Helens at the end of the 91/92 season when his contract was due to run out. McLennan had threatened to quit at the end of the 90/91 season and then changed his mind.

Look-A-Like

Your eyes would not have been deceiving you if you had thought Ellery Hanley was playing for the Sheffield Eagles. The Ex-GB U21 player, Anthony Farrell, who looked like the Great Britain captain, took to the field sporting a similar hair cut.

Where to?

As the end of season came into view, rumours about transfers abounded. Hot on the list was ex-Great Britain scrum-half Bobby Goulding who had reportedly been offered to Leeds by Wigan. Goulding was said to be keen to start playing first team rugby again after his showing for the Great Britain team on tour last year.

Pirates on the Look Out

One of the first players to be named for the Leagues' newest recruits, Scarborough, was their club captain, Peter Smith. Smith, aged 35, had been a stalwart at Featherstone, and had a long association with the Pirates' coach, Len Casey.

March 30th - April 5th

RESULTS

CHALLENGE CUP - Semi-final

St Helens 19	Widnes 2	

DIVISION 1

Castleford 14	Hull 16 bh	
Oldham 4	Wigan 10 bh	
Sheffield 62	Hull KR 16	
St Helens 12	Widnes 20 bh	
Wakefield 14	Leeds 14 bh	
Wigan 28	St Helens 14	mw

DIVISION 2

Batley 8	Huddersfield 18 bh	
Bramley 8	Fulham 8 bh	
Bramley 6	Workington 18 mw	
Carlisle 5	Workington 12 bh	
Carlisle 28	Trafford 0 mw	
Dewsbury 0	Halifax 26 bh	
Dewsbury 64	Nottingham 0 mw	
Halifax 42	Swinton 14 mw	
Hunslet 6	Ryedale-York 20 bh	
Leigh 42	Runcorn 6 bh	
Nottingham 12	Barrow 30 bh	
Runcorn 54	Keighley 16	
Swinton 10	Salford 10 bh	
Trafford 21	Chorley 19 bh	

	P	Pts
Widnes	23	36
Hull	24	34
Wigan	21	33
Castleford	24	32
Leeds	24	28
St Helens	24	25
Bradford	23	24
Featherstone	24	23
Hull KR	26	21
Warrington	24	20
Wakefield	24	20
Oldham	24	18
Sheffield	24	16
Rochdale	24	2

	P	Pts
Salford	26	49
Halifax	26	44
Ryedale-York	27	42
Swinton	26	42
Workington	26	35
Leigh	25	33
Fulham	25	32
Doncaster	25	30
Carlisle	25	30
Whitehaven	26	26
Huddersfield	25	25
Hunslet	26	24
Keighley	25	22
Trafford	26	20

ROUNDUP

The *Saints* came marching home with a resounding defeat of *Widnes* in the second semi-final of the Challenge Cup, played at Wigan. Jonathan Davies missed two early penalties for Widnes, but St Helens opened the scoring when Paul Loughlin kicked a penalty. Three tries and a late drop goal for the Saints were only matched by a half time penalty kick from Widnes.

In the only First Division Easter Sunday fixture, *Sheffield Eagles* showed that they are not planning on playing Second Division rugby just yet. Roger Millward, *Hull's* coach for 17 years, had hoped his farewell would be a happy occasion but instead Hull were greeted by a four try frenzy from the Eagles early in the second half. New Zealander Sam Panapa had a hat-trick of tries in his farewell match for the Eagles.

Bank Holiday Monday was a dismal day weather wise for spectators, but *Hull* managed to keep their championship dreams alive by beating *Castleford* despite having been 14-10 down until the final minutes. *Widnes* got revenge for their Challenge Cup defeat to stay top of the league by beating *St Helens*. *Wigan* remained in championship contention by beating *Oldham* despite the sending off of Kelvin Skerrett who had only just returned from injury. *Wakefield* came close to gaining revenge against *Leeds* in a repeat of Good Friday's fixture. The late sin binning of two Leeds players brought exciting play, with Wakefield making a last minute try to bring a draw at the final whistle.

74

No Second Division Holiday

Swinton drew with *Salford* after a last minute touchline goal kick could have given them victory but instead a draw clinched the championship for Salford. *Halifax* overpowered *Dewsbury* with four tries in the first half. *Ryedale-York* continued their attack on promotion with a 20-6 win over *Hunslet*. *Fulham's* trip north gave them a well earned draw on a muddy *Bramley* ground when they touched down with just four minutes of the game remaining. *Halifax* prepared to go up with Salford after a defiant win against championship rivals *Swinton*.

Who Gives A Toss

St Helens won the toss for the Challenge Cup Final which meant they could wear their own kit on the big day. Wigan were doomed to appear in their unfamiliar blue hooped kit. Jim Smith from Halifax was selected to make his Wembley debut, as referee.

Wellington's Winfield Cup Hopes

Salford's promotion winning coach Kevin Tamati was targeted by his old New Zealand club, Wellington, to bring them honours. The Kiwi Club, due to play in the Australian's Winfield Cup from 1993, hoped Tamati would help them meet their new challenge.

Yorkshire Sevens

Scarborough Pirates said they would announce their arrival into the League by holding a Sevens tournament at the end of the season. They hoped it would become an annual event.

Championship Trouble

Widnes and Wigan were battling to gain any advantage they could to ensure they would win the league. Widnes asked the League if they could change the date they were due to play Wigan from April 9th to April 11th. However Wigan have said their current existing fixture arrangement, whereby they were due to play Widnes on 9th April and Bradford on 11th, was better. The League agreed with Wigan.

Leigh Headache
Despite rumours that the club was about to appoint a receiver, Leigh carried on with business as usual.

Alliance Champions

Bradford Northern's 'A' team won the Slalom Lager Alliance Challenge Cup Final, beating Castleford 25-4. Although Northern 'A' were a Second Division side they had to take on the Alliance leagues' First Division teams to claim their title. They have also gained promotion to the first division next season.

April 6th - April 12th

RESULTS

DIVISION 1

Bradford 28	Hull 16
Featherstone 20	Leeds 52
Rochdale 6	Wakefield 25 mw
Sheffield 13	Widnes 18
Wakefield 8	St Helens 22
Warrington 22	Oldham 14
Wigan 24	Castleford 4
Wigan 26	Widnes 6 mw
Wigan 18	Bradford 18 mw

DIVISION 2

Barrow 26	Whitehaven 16
Batley 10	Hunslet 14
Bramley 17	Carlisle 12
Carlisle 24	Doncaster 8 mw
Chorley 6	Dewsbury 26
Dewsbury 20	Chorley 24 mw
Fulham 6	Doncaster 12
Fulham 28	Keighley 16 mw
Halifax 66	Trafford 26
Halifax 24	Leigh 18 mw
Huddersfield 20	Bramley 0 mw
Keighley 14	Swinton 10
Leigh 26	Huddersfield 13
Runcorn 42	Nottingham 0
Trafford 12	Salford 40 mw
Workington 12	Ryedale-York 6

	P	Pts
Wigan	25	40
Widnes	25	38
Hull	25	34
Castleford	25	32
Leeds	25	30
St Helens	25	27
Bradford	25	27
Featherstone	25	23
Warrington	25	22
Wakefield	26	22
Hull KR	26	21
Oldham	25	18
Sheffield	25	16
Rochdale	25	2

	P	Pts
Salford	27	51
Halifax	28	48
Ryedale-York	28	42
Swinton	27	42
Workington	27	37
Leigh	27	35
Fulham	27	34
Doncaster	27	32
Carlisle	27	32
Huddersfield	27	27
Hunslet	27	26
Whitehaven	27	26
Keighley	27	24
Dewsbury	27	20

ROUNDUP

A late interception by *Widnes* stole a planned move try from the *Eagles* to take them to victory and keep them top of the table at the weekend. For most of the game, relegated Sheffield looked at least the equals of the leaders.

    Leeds had a try-for-all day in a heavy defeat of *Featherstone* where both side's defences seemed non existent. Phil Ford took three tries while John Gallagher announced his return from injury with two and Simon Irving topped the points table with eight goals and one try.

    Wigan did not look a tired team as they ran *Castleford* in to the ground and kept the pressure on for their championship battle against Widnes two days later. *Northern* showed they could turn on class rugby when needed and secured a Premiership place by defeating *Hull*. Brett Iti continued his try scoring streak with another two and Karl Fairbank earned man-of-the-match with his performance which included two tries. *Wakefield* disappointed their fans when they allowed *St Helens* to score four tries to their one in a defeat at Belle Vue.

Midweek Madness

Halifax's Australian centre Greg Austin took his team to victory with a double hat trick of tries against *Trafford* and brought himself level with Martin Offiah in the leagues list of top try scorers. *Keighley's* loan player from Castleford, Paul Mirfin, opened the scoring for them in their unexpected defeat of *Swinton. Ryedale-York* could have secured their place in the First Division with a win over *Workington*, and a 6-6 half time score looked promising. However in the second half, an early drop goal followed up by a try from Workington's Australian centre secured the home side a win and a place in the Second Division championship play offs. *Doncaster's* trip south netted them a hard earned win despite an early try from *Fulham. Runcorn Highfield* have proved that they were not hogging the bottom of the second division spot when they beat *Nottingham City* with eight tries and two drop goals.

Wigan Triumpant

On Tuesday the top of the table battle between *Widnes* and *Wigan* brought a crowd of 26,950 along to Central park to see the outcome. Frano Botica opened Wigan's scoring with an early penalty and he went on to kick a further four goals and score a try. Jonathan Davies snuck in a hard run try for Widnes and then Wigan replied with another penalty and a try to give them a half time score of 8-6. Three tries in the second half sealed victory for Wigan after a display of relentless and ferocious tackling.

On Thursday *Bradford* seemed on course to beat *Wigan* when they led by 18-2 just after half time. Then a late sin binning of Bradford's hooker, Glen Barraclough, for a high tackle on Andy Gregory let Wigan back in for a drawn match. Kelvin Skerrett's two tries looked to be his last of the season as he faced a 4-match ban for the sending off he received against Oldham.

Noble Out

Bradford's Brian Noble missed his first match of the season on Thursday when his team met Wigan. Noble had broken a bone in his left leg and was replaced by 'A' team player Glen Barraclough.

Whitehaven Misery

The clubs debts were reported to be into six figures, and the staff at the club were having their wages paid by two of the directors.

Big Spenders

Wigan and Leeds were reported to be offering Australian Greg Alexander in the region of £150,000. His contract with Sydney Club Penrith was up for renewal.

Shining Light

Heworth in York were the first amateur Rugby League side to have floodlights at their ground. They were first used to light up in their match against Dudley Hill.

Referee!

Halifax's final game of the season ended in uproar with a twenty man brawl. Referee Colin Morris had to have a police escort from the pitch.

April 13th - April 19th

RESULTS

DIVISION 1

Bradford 18	Featherstone 34
Castleford 28	Sheffield 10
Leeds 8	Wigan 20
Oldham 19	Hull 14
St Helens 62	Warrington 16
Widnes 44	Rochdale 20

DIVISION 2

Dewsbury 19	Barrow 19
Doncaster 10	Leigh 42
Fulham 24	Runcorn 14
Hunslet 15	Workington 14
Nottingham 17	Chorley 32
Salford 30	Keighley 0
Swinton 42	Huddersfield 18
Whitehaven 12	Carlisle 18

FINAL TABLES

	P	Pts
Wigan	26	42
Widnes	26	40
Hull	26	34
Castleford	26	34
Leeds	26	30
St Helens	26	29
Bradford	26	27
Featherstone	26	25
Warrington	26	22
Wakefield	26	22
Hull KR	26	21
Oldham	26	20
Sheffield	26	16
Rochdale	26	2

	P	Pts
Salford	28	53
Halifax	28	48
Swinton	28	44
Ryedale-York	28	42
Leigh	28	37
Workington	28	37
Fulham	28	36
Carlisle	28	34
Doncaster	28	32
Hunslet	28	28
Huddersfield	28	27
Whitehaven	28	26
Keighley	28	24
Dewsbury	28	21
Trafford	28	20
Batley	28	20
Barrow	28	18
Chorley	28	15
Bramley	28	15
Runcorn	28	7
Nottingham	28	4

ROUNDUP

Wigan took the Stones Bitter League championship for the second year in succession when they beat *Leeds* at Headingley. Bobby Goulding kicked his team into an early lead and looked likely to stay at Wigan. Dennis Betts became the only player to survive all of Wigan's 37 matches in the season and celebrated with a late try. Shaun Wane was Leed's man of the match in a game which showed little of their talents.

Featherstone showed *Bradford* the gaps in their defence when they went over with four fast tries early in the second half. Two of the tries came from interceptions, and Ian Smales stormed through with a hat trick. *Sheffield* were leading *Castleford* 8-6 at half time, but Lee Crooks led a second half push which resulted in four Castleford tries and a win. *St Helen's* were leading 18-6 at half time, but the sending off of *Warrington's* winger, Mark Forster after 35 minutes, opened the door for the Saints players who scored twelve tries in the game and pushed the Wires out of the Premiership. *Oldham* showed a fighting spirit and took a final First Division win against *Hull*. Hull had a second half try disallowed when the referee said the player was held up but then he allowed a try by Gary Nolan which appeared to have been knocked down. Jonathan Davies still looked on course to beat the *Widnes* club record of 316 points in a season, after the game at *Rochdale* in which he kicked six goals and got one try in his team's win.

Sad Farewell

Dewsbury said farewell to their Crown Flatt ground with a heart stopping last minute try and goal to equalise against *Barrow*. In 1991/92 they will share a ground with Batley before their new stadium is completed. *Swinton* earned promotion in front of a home crowd when they beat *Huddersfield* and Tommy Frodsham scored two interception tries. *Fulham* reached their highest Second Division position for approximately a decade with their win over *Runcorn*.

Three Is Not A Crowd

A second vote by all clubs in the Rugby League on Wednesday night confirmed a new structure for the league. The motion was carried by 21 votes to 14 creating a First Division of 14 teams, a Second Division of 8, and a new Third Division of 14 teams. The new structure was set to start from 1991/92 with the teams finishing 12th-14th in the First Division in 1990/91 going down, those finishing 1st-3rd in the Second Division going up, 4th-8th remaining, and the rest starting in the Third with new member Scarborough. The new format scheduled for two clubs from each division to go up and down at the end of the season.

Tuffs Back

Simon Tuffs' appeal to the Rugby League against his ban to testing positive for amphetamine was upheld. Witnesses came forward to confirm Tuffs' statement that his drink had been spiked at a party. The League were able to reclaim a clean record since random drug testing was introduced four seasons ago.

Injury Time

Widnes feared that Martin Offiah would be unable to play in the first round of the Premiership after sustaining a thigh injury. Wigan had seven players receiving treatment at a London Clinic, and all were uncertain for Sunday's Premiership fixture but likely to be fit for Wembley. Kelvin Skerrett's appeal against his four match ban after an elbow incident against Oldham was not upheld, so ending his hopes of playing at Wembley.

Oldham

Forward Peter Tunks was tipped to be Oldham's next coach in a move from Sheffield Eagles. Tim Wilby looked likely to be his assistant, making him a busy man since he was also made manager of Oldham's greyhound stadium.

Cas Kiwi

Castleford signed New Zealander forward Tawera Nikau on a three year contract. Nikau had a spell playing for Rochdale Hornets earlier in the season.

April 20th - April 26th

RESULTS

DIVISION 1 PREMIERSHIP - Round 1

Castleford 20	Leeds 24
Hull 28	St Helens 12
Widnes 46	Bradford Northern 10
Wigan 26	Featherstone 31

DIVISION 2 PREMIERSHIP - Round 1

Halifax 42	Fulham 24
Ryedale-York 6	Leigh 11
Salford 26	Carlisle 12
Swinton 12	Workington 19

ROUNDUP

Castleford fans were already cheering their team's victory when Garry Schofield crept across the line to score a match winning injury time try for *Leeds*. In a game where the referee made no friends on either side both teams battled for the full 80 minutes. Castleford's early try from John Joyner got the home crowd cheering having just seen their stand-off, Graham Steadman, carried off with concussion and whiplash. Minutes later Garry Schofield appeared to go through with a superb interception try which was then disallowed by referee Jim Smith as a knock on. At half time Smith took the unprecedented step of apologising to the Leeds coach for his mistake. In the second half Leeds seemed to have the game in their pocket when Castleford came back with two tries in six minutes to take an 18-16 lead.

A half-time score of 6-6 did not reflect the battling that had taken place on the pitch as *St Helens* attacked for the full 40 minutes. Only excellent defending by *Hull* kept the Saints from running away with the game. In the second half Hull came back at the Saints to score three tries to their one. Paul Eastwood kicked six goals and Paul Loughlin two.

Widnes showed their home crowd that they intended to win the Premiership again with a trouncing of the previous year's fellow finalists *Bradford Northern*. Northern were without their recent stand off Bob Grogan who had to return to Australia, and despite some good bouts of play they were well beaten. Jonathan Davies passed the club's points record of 316, held for 12 years by Mick Burke, by scoring two tries and kicking five goals.

Wigan's chances of doing the 'triple' disappeared thanks to some inspired kicking by *Featherstone's* Deryck Fox. A young Wigan side, missing 11 of the players expected to be on show in the Challenge Cup Final were no match for the hard hitting experience of the Yorkshire side. Wigan's 80 second lead from a Kevin Iro try was evened up by a try from hooker Trevor Clark. Two substitutions after 45 minutes gave Featherstone the strength they needed to score two tries and take a 31-14 lead. Wigan came fighting back with tries from Steve Blakeley and Ian Gildart converted by Sean Tyrer, but it wasn't enough to stop Featherstone's 18th consecutive win.

Halifax scored eight tries to *Fulham's* four to put themselves in the next round. Greg Austin the Second Division's most prolific try scorer failed to make a mark in this match, enabling teammate and winger Martin Wood to take over and score four of his team's tries.

Scarborough FC's ground proved more inspiring for *Leigh* when they took a 10 point lead against *Ryedale-York* whose home ground was unavailable.

Salford did not have an easy win against *Carlisle* and it was only a 72nd minute try from Australian full back Steve Gibson that gave them their place in the next round.

Newly promoted *Swinton* were completely out run by *Workington Town* in the second half when Workington took 17 points without reply.

First Division Excluded

Stephen Ball the Chairman of Batley called for a separate competition for Second and Third Division teams, with the final to be held at Wembley.

Batley

Chairman of Batley, Stephen Ball, announced the departure of coach Keith Rayne after a disappointing performance by the club in the league. The club was going to have to get itself out of the newly formed Third Division at the first attempt, he said.

Hanley Hand-out

Ellery Hanley pledged a £6,000 libel settlement to charity. In private discussions with a newspaper the sum was agreed; £2,000 to go to the Wigan scanner appeal; £2,000 to the "Fight for Sight" appeal and £2,000 to the Rugby League Foundation for the development of junior Rugby League.

Spending Spree Stopped

Clubs were facing a ceiling on the amount they can spend on buying overseas players. The Rugby League said it would like to keep some of this £2 million business in the country to promote the game, and a discussion document outlined the proposal. The proposals meant First Division clubs would be limited to paying £60,000 per annum, Second Division clubs £30,000 and Third Division clubs £20,000, for foreign services.

Young Good-bye

After playing only eight matches for Leeds, forward David Young signed for Second Division Champions, Salford, for an undisclosed fee. Young, an ex-Welsh Rugby Union player joined Leeds fourteen months previously for a record £165,000 on a five year contract.

Oldham Troubles

Contract troubles still abounded at Oldham with two more players, centre Des Foy and forward Richard Russell, joining five others who had refused to sign new contracts.

April 27th - May 3rd

RESULTS

Wigan 13   St Helens 8

ROUNDUP

Wigan set off with a storming points scoring run straight from the kick off. They scored 12 points in as many minutes at the start of the game and the *St Helens* crowd must have thought that the match was going to be a whitewash. An early penalty was awarded after George Mann dived on to a knocked-on ball from the scrum and Shane Cooper challenged the referee's decision. Mr Smith is known for not taking "talk" from players, and the penalty was converted by Frano Botica. Wigan went on to score their first try almost straight away after Saint's full back Phil Veivers collided with opposition player Shaun Edwards and the ball went free. Kevin Iro picked up the ball, passed to David Myers and he was over before Saints could recover. Frano Botica kicked for his second goal of the match. Their second try came along too quickly for the Saints when a Paul Loughlin kick failed to find touch, Wigan's possession then saw Dean Bell pass to man-of-the-match Dennis Betts and on to Frano Botica to go over. Botica then converted as has been his usual consistent play all season. This dominating opening from Wigan did not stop Saint's forwards battling for possession and control of the game. Led by John Harrison and Bernard Dwyer they fought for every opportunity but Wigan did not give them many.

Early in the second half Andy Gregory edged Wigan forward with a drop goal. Twenty minutes later Andy Goodway messed up a pass; Phil Veivers and Harrison saw the opportunity and kept the ball moving before Jonathan Griffiths sent a high pass over to Allan Hunte at the far corner for the Saints first try. Paul Bishop converted and scored again with a penalty kick, leaving an exciting last 10 minutes with everything to be played for. However, Wigan kept the Saints out, and some more mistakes from St Helens meant that Wigan could rightfully claim their fourth successive Challenge Cup title. Saints' Chairman, Eric Latham, commented that his team had been in the game for 68 minutes, but Wigan had shown what they can do when given just 12 minutes.

Iro Back

Kevin Iro left Wigan for Australia to play with his brother, Tony, for top club Manly. Wigan still hoped he would return to Central Park for 1991/92, but Iro stated that he would need a rest after the Australian season and that he was planning to make his future in Australia.

British Sevens

A proposed sevens tournament was proposed to be held in Australia with eight invitation teams, one of which would be Great Britain.

Highfield

Runcorn Highfield announced that they would be called Highfield RFC from 1991/92 in their seventh name change since the club was formed in 1922.

May 4th - May 10th

RESULTS

FIRST DIVISION PREMIERSHIP
Semi Final

| Hull 10 | Leeds 7 |
| Widnes 42 | Featherstone 28 |

SECOND DIVISION PREMIERSHIP
Semi Final

| Halifax 32 | Leigh 7 |
| Salford 9 | Workington 9 |

ROUNDUP

Hull looked like they were going out of the cup to *Leeds* when a last minute expert "bomb" kick from Greg Mackey was knocked from the grasp of full back John Gallagher and newly substituted Gary Nolan was able to fall on to it for a match winning try. Hull had missed early chances to score when Leeds had kept them from the line three times in the opening minutes. Garry Schofield opened the scoring for Leeds with a drop goal after twenty minutes of play. Leed's try was a masterpiece of support play and running rugby with Richard Gunn the man to go over the line. Hull's only other points came from two penalty kicks.

Widnes stormed to an early lead over *Featherstone* who came back in an action filled second half. Widnes were leading by thirty points just after half time but then Featherstone started to fight back. Their three tries in the last quarter of an hour was not enough to keep Widnes from their fourth consecutive Premiership final.

Halifax became the only Yorkshire side to make it to a Premiership final when they beat *Leigh* for the third time in the season. Halifax opened the scoring, and their relentless attacking of a strong Leigh defence paid dividends in the end. Greg Austin scored two tries, taking his season's tally to 47.

Workington forced a replay with *Salford* at Derwent Park to decide who would meet Halifax in the final. A last minute drop goal from stand off, Stephen Wear, kept Workington in the reckoning. The teams were level at 8-8 at half time, and the second half saw hooker Mark Lee put a drop goal over to edge Salford in to the lead.

Papua on Tour

Papua New Guinea's Rugby League players were scheduled to come over to the UK in October 1991. Their opening match was programmed to be against a resurrected Welsh team which had not been seen on a field since 1984. The match was set for Swansea City's Vetch Field ground on 27th October. The tourists other four matches were scheduled to be against the Great Britain under 21's at Headingley, a Humberside Select at The Boulevard, and a Cumbria team. Wigan was picked for their Test match as the tourists fourth and final game on November 9th.

Player of the Year

Jonathan Davies crowned his second year of Rugby League by being voted First Division Player of the Year by his fellow professionals. Davies was still fighting a back injury to be fit for the Premiership final. Tawera Nikau was voted Second Division Player of the Year. Garry Schofield was voted Stones Bitter Man of Steel for his contribution to the game over the previous twelve months.

May 11th - May 17th

RESULTS

FIRST DIVISION PREMIERSHIP
Final

SECOND DIVISION PREMIERSHIP
Final

Hull 14   Widnes 4   Halifax 20   Salford 27

ROUNDUP

Hull surprised all but their own supporters when they won the Premiership Final for the first time in the club's history. *Widnes* were never given the chance to run and play their style of open rugby as Hull's defence kept them locked in their own half. The Hull forwards however were able to keep up relentless pressure, allowing their team to take control and score the winning tries. Many thought the half time score of 8-0 to Hull would not last long in the second half, and Widnes looked set to take revenge when Martin Offiah scored his spectacular 49th try of the season. However 10 minutes later, troublesome newcomer Gary Nolan defied the grapples of three Widnes players to reach out and put down the ball for Hull's third and winning try. Six weeks previously Nolan was playing amateur rugby but he had joined his brother at Hull with two match winning tries. Paul Eastwood converted, having missed two earlier conversions and a penalty. Hull's Australian captain Greg Mackey was voted man-of-the-match for his clever play and searching kicks.

Halifax looked set to make it a Yorkshire first in the Premiership but two last quarter errors gave victory to local Lancastrians *Salford*. Halifax were leading 10-6 at half time and then, when they were up 16-14, Roy Southernwood lost the ball which was quickly snapped up by Tex Evans for a try. At 21-16, a tangle of players cleared the way for Mike Dean to retrieve a loose ball and pass it to John Gilfillan to go in for his try. Steve Kerry converted, and took his tally of points for the match to 17 to win the Tom Bergin Trophy for man-of-the-match. Halifax did not give up, and in the 76th minute Martin Woods scored a try. The last few minutes of the match were marred by a brawl which continued after the final whistle had gone. Bradford referee Brian Galtress said he could not single out any particular players for punishment. Greg Austin did not manage to increase his tally of tries despite making the break to give Halifax their third try.

Laughton Off

Doug Laughton surprised the Rugby League world by announcing he was leaving Widnes to join Leeds as manager. Laughton had long envied the buying power of clubs such as Leeds and Wigan. Leeds' existing coach David Ward was asked to work along side the new manager but he declined. Leeds refuted Widnes' claim that they poached Laughton, saying that he had told Widnes of his intention to leave at the end of the season some weeks previously.

Widnes Keep Hold

Martin Offiah was refused an early release from his ten year contract with Widnes which still had 6 years to run.

Bad Show

Some Widnes players who did not climb the steps to the guests of honour to receive their runners-up medals at the Premiership Final were told they could expect to be reprimanded by the league.

Top Ref
John Holdsworth was voted referee of the year for the fourth year by the players. He received his award on the pitch prior to the Premiership Final at Old Trafford.

Down Under
The flights to Australia and New Zealand had their fair share of British players on them. Martin Offiah and team mate Andy Currier set off to play for St George in Sydney. Jonathan Davies went off to play for Canterbury, Emosi Koloto for Sydney, Daryl Powell for Gold Coast and Kevin Iro for Manly.

Back in the USSR
Ryedale-York and Fulham set off for an historic inaugural tour of the Soviet Union. They went to play exhibition matches in Alma Ata and Leningrad, and then combine to play the national rugby team at Dynamo Stadium in Moscow on 23rd May.

Stones Stay
Stones Bitter said they will be sponsoring the 1991-92 season in a deal worth £2 million over the next five years.

1990/1991 Stones Bitter Championship

Top Ten Try Scorers

1.	Martin Offiah (Widnes)	49
2.	Greg Austin (Halifax)	47
3.	Martin Wood (Halifax)	31
4.	Jonathan Davies (Widnes)	30
	Adrian Hadley (Salford)	30
6.	Ellery Hanley (Wigan)	29
7.	Alan Hunte (St Helens)	26
	Les Quirk (St Helens)	26
9.	Garry Schofield (Leeds)	25
10.	Andy Currier (Widnes)	23
	John Devereux (Widnes)	23
	Graham Steadman (Cas)	23

Top Ten Goal Scorers

1.	Steve Kerry (Salford)	177
2.	Frano Botica (Wigan)	126
3.	Paul Eastwood (Hull)	119
4.	Jonathan Davies (Widnes)	112
5.	Simon Irving (Leeds)	99
6.	Graham Sullivan (Ryedale)	94
	Paul Louglin (St Helens)	94
8.	Alan Platt (Halifax)	91
9.	Barry Vickers (Carlisle)	88
10.	Tim Lumb (Hunslet)	85

TOP FIVE POINT SCORERS

1. Steve Kerry (Salford)		423
2. Jonathan Davies (Widnes)		342
3. Frano Botica (Wigan)		324
4. Paul Eastwood (Hull)		294
5. Simon Irving (Leeds)		242

Offiah's Offerings

Martin Offiah declared he would not play for Widnes unless the terms of his contract were renegotiated. It was said that if Offiah was not playing for Widnes then it was very unlikely he would be available for International duties. Offiah was playing for St George in Australia whilst his future in Britain was being decided.

Halifax Hopes

Hull's coach Roger Millward agreed a move to newly promoted Halifax, and Alan Agar, who left Rochdale in January, was appointed his second in command.

Friday Fixtures

The Great Britain tour to Australia in 1992 was scheduled to have the test matches played on a Friday. The planned fixtures were for Sydney on June 12th and July 3rd, and Brisbane on June 26th. Club matches were planned to include the Illawarra Steelers on 8th June and the Gold Coast Giants on 23rd June.

Farewell

Australian winger Brian Bevan, who played for Warrington, died in Blackpool aged 66 on 3rd June. In his career he scored a World Record 796 tries between 1945 and 1964 and was often referred to as the best Rugby League player of all time.

Wigan Win

Andy Gregory turned down an approach from Widnes to be player coach for the following season, by signing a 12 month contract with Wigan. Wally Lewis and Peter Sterling also turned down coaching offers from Widnes.

Union Money

The England players proposal for a £2 million promotion package was turned down by the other Home Countries. The scheme 'Run with the Ball' had been approved by the English Rugby Union. The players said they would not earn any money from the promotion, its aim was to harness business money for the Union game.

Wigan Lose

Mark Preston, Wigan's winger, joined Halifax for an undisclosed fee.

Test for Kiwis

New Zealand beat France by their highest score ever, 66-6 in Auckland. Frano Botica, in his first outing as a Rugby League player in his home country, kicked eight conversions.

Good On Yer

English players were earning their money down under. Martin Offiah of Widnes had scored five tries in four matches for St George; Jonathan Davies of Wigan clinched victory for Canterbury with a last minute try after a 50 metre dash; Dave Myers of Wigan scored on his return to the Manly first team.

Colts Clash

The two governing bodies of Rugby League, The Rugby Football League (Professional) and BARLA (Amateur) could not agree on who should manage Colts Rugby. BARLA had run it for the previous three years, but the Football league proposed the setting up of an under-18 league. It was uncertain whether players from this league would still be entitled to play as amateurs.

Leigh Low Point

The creditors of Leigh Rugby League club allowed the administrator more time to find a buyer. The club had debts of over £1 million. One proposal was on the table to buy the club, but not their Hilton Park ground. The club would then share nearby Station Road currently used by Swinton.

New Kit

Umbro agreed £500,000 worth of sponsorship for the Rugby League. This meant new International Kit and a £10,000 bonus if Great Britain beat Australia in the series next year.

More Money

It was announced that £17 million was likely to be received by Rugby League over the next five years from sponsors and television. The Rugby League's board of directors said this unprecedented injection of income had resulted from skilled negotiations over the years. The money was set to come almost equally from sponsors and from TV rights. £25,000 was going to be used to promote the game in the Soviet Union, and it was hoped that Australia would donate the same amount.

No Credit

Highfield, formerly known as Runcorn Highfield beat many of their First Division peers by turning in a profit for the season. Despite a record breaking run of 77 games without a win the club made a profit of £69,600.

Ooh La Ouch!

French International centre David Fraisse was involved in a motorcycle accident just days before he was due to sign for Castleford. The gifted young player was left in a coma after the accident and has sustained injuries to his head, a broken collar bone and broken ribs.

African Visit

It was announced that Castleford's Chairman, David Poulter, will be making a visit to South Africa to see the potential for Rugby League development in this strong Rugby Union country.

Amnesty

The Australian Rugby Union authorities were contemplating an amnesty for League players. They said it wasn't going to solve the problem of losing players to League, but it would encourage more players back to club level. The executive director of the New South Wales RFU, Gary Pearse, the former Australian flanker, said he would like to see ex-league players allowed to play club level Rugby for either code.

Widnes Signing

Frank Myler, who was associated with Widnes during their winning days in the Seventies, was appointed coach. Myler had a successful playing career with Widnes and had coached the International side. His last post was coach at Oldham, which he left in 1987.

The Rugby Football League - Main Fixture Dates

1991

August 25	CIS Insurnace Charity Shield: Wigan v Hull (at Gateshead)
September 1	Stones Bitter Championship season starts
September 15	County Cup competitions (1st round)
September 18	Rodstock War of the Roses: Yorkshire v Lancashire (at Headingley, Leeds)
September 25	County Cup competitions (2nd round)
October 2	Foster's World Cup Challenge (at Old Trafford, Manchester)
October 9	County Cup competitions semi-finals
October 19	Lancashire Cup Final
October 20	John Smith's Yorkshire Cup Final
October 27	Wales v Papua New Guinea (at Vetch Field, Swansea)
October 30	Great Britain U-21 v Papua New Guinea (at Headingley)
November 3	Humberside v Papua New Guinea (at The Boulevard, Hull)
November 5	Cumbria v Papua New Guinea
November 9	British Coal Test: Great Britain v Papua New Guinea (at Central Park, Wigan)
November 16/17	Regal Trophy (1st round)
November 23/24	Regal Trophy (2nd round)
December 1	Regal Trophy (3rd round)
December 7	Regal Trophy (Semi-final)
December 21	Regal Trophy (Semi-final)

1992

January 11	Regal Trophy Final
January 25/26	Silk Cut Challenge Cup (1st round)
February 8/9	Silk Cut Challenge Cup (2nd round)
February 22/23	Silk Cut Challenge Cup (3rd round)
March 14	Silk Cut Challenge Cup (Semi-final)
March 28	Silk Cut Challenge Cup (Semi-final)
April 21	Stones Bitter Divisional Premiership (1st round)*
April 26	Stones Bitter Premiership (1st round)
	Stones Bitter Divisional Premiership (2nd round)
May 2	Silk Cut Challenge Cup Final (at Wembley)
May 10	Stones Bitter Premiership Semi-final
	Stones Bitter Divisional Premiership Semi-final
May 17	Stones Bitter Premiership Final
	Stones Bitter Divisional Premiership Final (at Old Trafford, Manchester)

*The new Stones Bitter Divisional Premiership will be contested in the first round by the top eight teams in the Third Division. The four winners will then join the top four clubs from the Second Division for the second round. Great Britain v France tests and U-21 Internationals to be announced.

Lions Tour 1992

Wednesday	3 June	Queensland County, Townsville
Saturday	6 June	Brisbane Broncos Long Park, Brisbane
Monday	8 June	Gold Coast Seagulls, Tweed Heads
Friday	12 June	AUSTRALIA - 1st test, Sydney
Tuesday	16 June	NSW Country, Parkes
Friday	19 June	Canberra Raiders, Bruce Stadium
Tuesday	23 June	Illawarra Steelers, Wollongong
Friday	26 June	AUSTRALIA 2nd test, Long Park, Brisbane
Tuesday	30 June	Newcastle Knights, Newcastle
Friday	3 July	AUSTRALIA - 3rd Test, Sydney
Tuesday	7 July	TBA
Sunday	12 July	NEW ZEALAND - 1st test
Tuesday	14 July	TBA
Sunday	19 July	NEW ZEALAND - 2nd Test

CLUB ADDRESSES
FIRST DIVISION

Bradford Northern
Odsal Stadium,
Bradford BD6 1BS
Tel:0274 733899

Castleford
Wheldon Road,
Castleford, WF10 2SD
Tel: 0977 552674

Featherstone Rovers
Post Office Road,
Featherstone
Tel: 0977 702386

Halifax
The Pavilion, Thrum Hall,
Gibbet Street, Halifax
Tel: 0422 361026

Hull
The Boulevard, Airlie Street,
Hull HU3 3JD
Tel: 0482 29040

Hull Kingston Rovers
Craven Park, Preston Road, Hull
HU9 5HE
Tel: 0482 74648

Leeds
Headingley, St Michael's Lane,
Leeds LS6 3BR
Tel: 0532 31321

St Helens
Knowsley Road,
St Helens
Tel: 0744 23697

Salford
The Willows, Willows Road,
Weaste, Salford M5 2FT
Tel: 061 737 6363

Swinton
Station Road, Swinton, Manchester
M27 1DD
Tel: 061 794 1719

Wakefield Trinity
Belle Vue, Doncaster Road,
Wakefield WF1 5HT
Tel: 0924 372445

Warrington
Wilderspool Stadium,
Warrington WA4 6PY
Tel: 0925 35338

Widnes
Naughton Park, Loerhouse Lane,
Widnes WA8 7DZ
Tel: 051 495 2250

Wigan
The Pavilion, Central Park,
Wigan WN1 1XF
Tel: 0942 31321

SECOND DIVISION

Carlisle
Gillford Park, Petteril Bank Rd,
Carlisle, CA3 9AB
Tel: 0228 401212

Fulham
Crystal Palace Sports Centre,
Leadington Road, London SE19
Tel:081 659 4241

Leigh
Hilton Park,
Leigh
Tel: 0942 674437

Oldham
The Watersheddings,
Oldham OL4
Tel: 061 624 4865

Rochdale Hornets
Spotland Stadium, Sandy Lane,
Rochdale, OL11 5DS
Tel: 0706 48004

Ryedale-York
RyedaleStadium,
Jockey Lane, Huntington, York
Tel: 0904 644636

Sheffield Eagles
Don Valley Stadium, Attercliffe Rd,
Sheffield
Tel: 0742 337664

Workington Town
Derwent Park,
Workington
Tel: 0900 603609

THIRD DIVISION

Barrow
Craven Park, Duke Street,
Barrow-in-Furness, LA14 5UW
Tel: 0229 820273

Batley
Mount Pleasant,
Batley
Tel: 0924 472208

Bramley
McLaren Field, Town Street,
Leeds LS13
Tel: 0532 564842

Chorley
Victory Park, Duke Street,
Chorley PR7
Tel: 02572 63406

Dewsbury
(Sharing Batley ground)

Doncaster
Tattersfield, Bentley Road,
Doncaster
Tel: 0302 390150

Highfield
439 Clockface Rd, St Helens,
Merseyside WA9 4Q
Tel: 09285 60076

Huddersfield
Fartown, Huddersfield
HB2 2SD
Tel: 0484 530710

Hunslet
Elland Road,
Leeds
Tel: 0532 711675

Keighley
Lawkholme Lane,
Keighley
Tel: 0535 602602

Nottingham City
Harvey Haddon Stadium, Wigman Rd,
Bilborough, Nottingham
Tel: 0602 691666

Scarborough Pirates
McCain Stadium, Seamer Rd,
Scarborough WO12 4HS
Tel:0723 375094

Trafford Borough
Altrincham AFC, Moss Lane,
Altrincham
Tel: 061 926 9844

Whitehaven
Recreation Ground, Coach Road,
Whitehaven
Tel: 0946 692915

1991/92 Stones Bitter Championship - 1st Division

FIXTURES	Bradford	Castleford	Featherstone	Halifax	Hull	Hull KR	Leeds
Bradford		3rd Nov	8th Mar	26th Dec	5th Jan	1st Sep	6th Oct
Castleford	19th Jan		27th Oct	10th Nov	26th Dec*	8th Dec	22nd Sep
Featherstone	29th Sep	15th Mar		5th Jan	13th Oct	1st Mar	15th Dec
Halifax	1st Jan	12th Apr	1st Sep		1st Dec	20th Oct	20th Apr
Hull	20th Oct	20th Apr	8th Dec	2nd Feb		1st Jan	22nd Mar
Hull KR	20th Apr	13th Oct	19th Jan	8th Sep	17th Apr		16th Feb
Leeds	8th Dec	2nd Feb	10th Nov	17th Apr**	8th Sep	26/29th Dec#	
St Helens	13th Oct	29th Sep	12th Jan	22nd Mar	29th Mar	10th Nov	1st Mar
Salford	28th Feb	8th Sep	16th Feb	13th Oct	27th Oct	12th Apr	19th Jan
Swinton	15th Mar	15th Dec	22nd Mar	12th Jan	5th Apr	6th Oct	1st Dec
Wakefield	8th Sep	1st Jan	20th Apr	8th Mar	29th Sep	12th Jan	20th Oct
Warrington	10th Nov	20th Oct	22nd Sep	8th Dec	16th Feb	8th Mar	5th Jan
Widnes	22nd Mar	5th Jan	20th Oct	1st Mar	19th Jan	22nd Sep	1st Sep
Wigan	12th Apr	1st Dec	6th Oct	27th Oct	15th Dec	2nd Feb	3rd Nov

All matches start at 3pm/3.15pm except those marked * which start at 11.30am; those marked ** start at 7.30pm;those marked # have yet to be confirmed.

St Helens	Salford	Swinton	Wakefield	Warrington	Widnes	Wigan	FIXTURES
2nd Feb	22nd Sep	17th Apr	5th Apr	15th Dec	1st Dec	12th Jan	**Bradford**
8th Mar	12th Jan	29th Mar	17th Apr**	1st Mar	6th Oct	1st Sep	**Castleford**
1st Dec	3rd Nov	8th Sep	26th Dec*	2nd Feb	29th Mar	5th Apr	**Featherstone**
6th Oct	15th Dec	16th Feb	22nd Sep	15th Mar	3rd Nov	19th Jan	**Halifax**
1st Sep	6th Oct	10th Nov	1st Mar	12th Jan	12th Apr	22nd Sep	**Hull**
15th Dec	1st Dec	5th Jan	27th Oct	29th Sep	15th Mar	29th Mar	**Hull KR**
27th Oct	1st Jan	29th Sep	29th Mar	13th Oct	12th Jan	15th Mar	**Leeds**
	20th Oct	8th Dec	19th Jan	8th Sep	1st Jan	17th Apr	**St Helens**
5th Jan		26 Dec	8th Dec	29th Mar	29th Sep	10th Nov	**Salford**
22nd Sep	20th Apr		1st Sep	3rd Nov	2nd Feb	20th Oct	**Swinton**
3rd Nov	2nd Feb	12th Apr		1st Dec	15th Dec	13th Oct	**Wakefield**
5th Apr	1st Sep	19th Jan	6th Oct		17th Apr	1st Jan	**Warrington**
20th Apr	5th Apr	13th Oct	10th Nov	26th Dec		8th Dec	**Widnes**
26th Dec	22nd Mar	1st Mar	5th Jan	20th Apr	8th Sep		**Wigan**

1991/92 Stones Bitter Championship - 2nd Division

FIXTURES	Carlisle	Fulham	Leigh	Oldham	Rochdale	Ryedale-York	Sheffield	Workington
Carlisle		13th Oct	10th Nov	20th Oct	12th Jan	8th Dec	8th Sep	29th Sep
Fulham	15th Dec		29th Sep	6th Oct	3rd Nov	20th Oct	22nd Sep	12th Jan
Leigh	22nd Sep	26th Dec		3rd Nov	8th Dec	1st Sep	13th Oct	20th Oct
Oldham	5th Jan	8th Dec	8th Sep		29th Sep	13th Oct	27th Oct	10th Nov
Rochdale	1st Sep	8th Sep	6th Oct	1st Dec		22nd Sep	5th Jan	15th Dec
Ryedale-York	6th Oct	8th Mar	27th Oct	15th Dec	10th Nov		29th Sep	8th Sep
Sheffield	3rd Nov	2nd Feb	15th Dec	1st Sep	20th Oct	29th Dec		6th Oct
Workington	1st Dec	1st Sep	5th Jan	22nd Sep	13th Oct	3rd Nov	8th Dec	

Carlisle	Fulham	Leigh	Oldham	Rochdale	Ryedale-York	Sheffield	Workington	FIXTURES
	23rd Feb	15th Mar	29th Mar	12th Apr	17th Apr	19th Jan	26th Dec	**Carlisle**
22nd Mar		1st Dec	16th Feb	19th Jan	5th Jan	10th Nov	1st Mar	**Fulham**
2nd Feb	29th Mar		1st Jan	5th Apr	12th Jan	23rd Feb	8th Mar	**Leigh**
8th Mar	15th Mar	20th Apr		26th Dec	23rd Jan	12th Jan	5th Apr	**Oldham**
1st Mar	20th Apr	16th Feb	17th Apr		2nd Feb	29th Mar	22nd Mar	**Rochdale**
16th Feb	5th Apr	1st Mar	12th Apr	15th Mar		26th Dec	19th Jan	**Ryedale-York**
5th Apr	12th Apr	22nd Mar	1st Mar	8th Mar	19th Apr		16th Feb	**Sheffield**
20th Apr	27th Oct	12th Apr	2nd Feb	23rd Feb	29th Mar	15th Mar		**Workington**

1991/92 Stones Bitter Championship - 3rd Division

FIXTURES	Barrow	Batley	Bramley	Chorley	Dewsbury	Doncaster	Highfield
Barrow		22nd Mar	13th Oct	12th Jan	8th Mar	8th Sep	29th Sep
Batley	6th Oct		16th Feb	3rd Nov	26th Dec*	8th Dec	12th Jan
Bramley	15th Dec	5th Apr		20th Oct	3rd Nov	1st Mar	22nd Mar
Chorley	22nd Sep	13th Oct	8th Dec		1st Sep	22nd Mar	29th Mar
Dewsbury	5th Jan	1st Jan	29th Sep	15th Dec		10th Nov	1st Mar
Doncaster	15th Mar	2nd Feb	27th Oct	1st Dec	22nd Sep		19th Jan
Highfield	1st Dec	27th Oct	8th Mar	23rd Feb	6th Oct	5th Apr	
Huddersfield	5th Apr	8th Sep	10th Nov	2nd Feb	8th Dec	29th Sep	13th Oct
Hunslet	1st Sep	1st Mar	26th Dec	5th Apr	20th Apr	16th Feb	20th Oct
Keighley	20th Oct	29th Sep	12th Jan	8th Sep	29th Mar	13th Oct	10th Nov
Nottingham	1st Mar	10th Nov	2nd Feb	15th Mar	12th Jan	29th Dec	8th Dec
Scarborough	2nd Feb	15th Dec	15th Mar	6th Oct	1st Dec	22nd Dec	1st Sep
Trafford	3rd Nov	17th Apr**	8th Sep	1st Jan	20th Oct	12th Jan	16th Feb
Whitehaven	29th Mar	19th Jan	17th Apr	29th Sep	16th Feb	20th Oct	8th Sep

All matches start at 3pm/3.15pm except those marked * which start at 11.30am; those marked ** start at 7.30pm;those marked # have yet to be confirmed.

Huddersfield	Hunslet	Keighley	Nottingham	Scarborough	Trafford	Whitehaven	FIXTURES
16th Feb	10th Nov	12th Apr	19th Jan	27th Oct	8th Dec	22nd Dec	**Barrow**
20th Oct	29th Mar	1st Dec	22nd Sep	8th Mar	20th Apr	1st Sep	**Batley**
22nd Sep	1st Jan	1st Sep	6th Oct	19th Jan	5th Jan	1st Dec	**Bramley**
5th Jan	27th Oct	19th Jan	16th Feb	10th Nov	26th Dec	1st Mar	**Chorley**
12th Apr	8th Sep	2nd Feb	22nd Mar	13th Oct	19th Jan	27th Oct	**Dewsbury**
3rd Nov	12th Apr	5th Jan	1st Sep	29th Mar	6th Oct	15th Dec	**Doncaster**
15th Dec	15th Mar	22nd Sep	3rd Nov	5th Jan	1st Sep	2nd Feb	**Highfield**
	17th Apr	1st Mar	8th Mar	29th Dec	27th Oct	12th Jan	**Huddersfield**
19th Jan		6th Oct	1st Dec	8th Dec	27th Sep	3rd Nov	**Hunslet**
20th Apr	15th Dec		23rd Feb	16th Feb	15th Mar	5th Apr*	**Keighley**
29th Mar	29th Sep	27th Oct		8th Sep	12th Apr	13th Oct	**Nottingham**
12th Apr	12th Jan	3rd Nov	20th Oct		1st Mar	22nd Sep	**Scarborough**
1st Dec	13th Oct	22nd Mar	15th Dec	29th Sep		8th Mar	**Trafford**
6th Oct	23rd Feb	8th Dec	5th Jan	22nd Mar	10th Nov		**Whitehaven**

97